MICKEY GILLEY'S TEXAS COOKBOOK

by Mickey Gilley

A WALLABY BOOK
Published by Simon & Schuster, Inc.
New York

Published by Wallaby Books
A Division of Simon & Schuster, Inc.
Simon & Schuster Building
1230 Avenue of the Americas
New York, New York 10020

Designed by Stanley S. Drate/Folio Graphics Co. Inc.

WALLABY and colophon are registered trademarks of Simon & Schuster, Inc.
First Wallaby Books printing June, 1984

10 9 8 7 6 5 4 3 2 1

Manufactured in the United States of America

Printed and bound by Command Web

Library of Congress Cataloging in Publication Data

Gilley, Mickey.
   Mickey Gilley's Texas cookbook.

   "A Wallaby book."
   1. Cookery, American—Texas. I. Title. II. Title: Texas cookbook. III. Title: Texas
cook book.
TX715.G49   1984   641.59764   84-3573

ISBN: 0-671-50487-8

Special thanks to—

Pat Wright
Irene Gilley
Maxine Gilley
Art LaRue
Neva Kauti
Mary Shields
Leon Beck

CONTENTS

Introduction

Texas—a state that has produced some great country music singers and some great country cooking. Although I am originally from Ferriday, Louisiana, my roots are now in Texas, and since moving here in the early '50s, I have been introduced to "Texas-style" cooking. Because of my love for Texas foods, I decided to share some of my favorite dishes with my fans and friends across the country who may not have been lucky enough to have been exposed to such delicious Texas foods.

In this cookbook are some of my favorite dishes—dishes that represent the finest in Lone Star State cooking. As an entertainer I travel on the road a lot, and I get to sample foods from almost all over the country. But there's nothing quite like Texas-flavored barbecue, chili, or the delicious Tex-Mex dishes.

It's not often that an entertainer has the opportunity to compile such a book, but thanks to the fine folks at Simon & Schuster, I have been given the opportunity to share a part of Texas with you. As you may know, I own a nightclub in Pasadena, Texas, called Gilley's. We have folks from all across the country and the world who visit this country music honky-tonk. They've always got a taste of the finest music in the country at Gilley's; now they've got the chance to taste Gilley's cookin' in their own kitchen.

1

SHOOT 'EM UP SOUPS AND SALADS

INDIAN SOUP

This dish offers a whole lot of good eatin' with very little effort. And it's mighty good for you.

1/4 cup margarine
  1 large yellow onion, sliced
  2 cans chicken broth
  1 can whole yellow corn
  1 can zucchini squash
  1 teaspoon salt
1/8 teaspoon black pepper
1/2 teaspoon cinnamon
  1 cup cream

1. Heat margarine and sauté onion until soft.
2. Add remaining ingredients, stir, and bring to low boil.
3. Reduce heat to low, and simmer for 10 minutes. Serve warm.

SERVES 4 TO 6

STAMPEDE CHICKEN SOUP

Set this bowl of hot steaming chicken soup in front of any tired cowboy, and his eyes will blaze like Fourth-of-July fireworks.

  2 tablespoons margarine
1/2 cup chopped yellow onion
  1 cup hot water
  2 cans chicken noodle soup
  1 can cream-style corn
1/4 teaspoon black pepper
  2 tablespoons dried parsley flakes

1. In medium pot heat margarine and sauté onions until soft.
2. Add remaining ingredients, stir, and bring to a boil. Serve warm.

SERVES 4 TO 6

SQUAW SOUP

Any cowboy will go on the warpath to sip this soup.

1/4 cup margarine
2 cups chopped green onions
3 cups diced potatoes
2 garlic cloves, chopped
4 cups beef broth
1 teaspoon salt
1/2 teaspoon black pepper
2 tablespoons Worcestershire sauce

1. In a large pot heat margarine and sauté onions, potatoes, and garlic at low heat until lightly browned.
2. Add remaining ingredients and bring to a boil.
3. Reduce heat to low, and simmer about 30 minutes until potatoes are soft. Serve warm.

SERVES 4 TO 6

POTATO-TOMATO SOUP

A soup so hearty you can scoop it up. Ideal to warm up cold nights—and cold hearts.

8 medium potatoes, peeled and sliced
6 large tomatoes, sliced
2 yellow onions, peeled and sliced
4 cups hot water
1/2 teaspoon crushed red (cayenne) pepper
1 bell pepper, sliced
1/2 teaspoon parsley flakes
1 tablespoon salt
1/2 teaspoon black pepper

1. Combine all ingredients in a pot and bring to a boil.
2. Reduce heat and simmer about 1 hour, until potatoes are tender.

SERVES 4 TO 6

SERVING SUGGESTION: *Delicious with Corral Corn Bread (page 130).*

STILL HUNTER'S SOUP

Surround a couple of squirrels with carrots, potatoes, corn, beans, and other good-tasting foods, and you've got a heck of a soup.

2 squirrels, cut in serving pieces
1/2 yellow onion, diced
1/4 cup margarine
1 cup diced celery
1 bell pepper, diced
2 teaspoons salt
1/2 teaspoon black pepper
6 cups water
1 16-ounce can whole-kernel corn
1 16-ounce can green lima beans
2 cups sliced potatoes
1 cup sliced carrots
1 16-ounce can stewed tomatoes (preferably Ro-tel)

1. Combine squirrels, onion, margarine, celery, bell pepper, seasonings, and water in a large stockpot and bring to a boil.
2. Reduce heat and simmer about 2 hours, until meat is tender (depending on age of squirrel).
3. Add remaining ingredients and return to a boil.
4. Reduce heat and simmer about 1 hour, until potatoes and carrots are tender.

SERVES 6 TO 8

SERVING SUGGESTION: *This soup is especially good with Corral Corn Bread (page 130).*

CHICKEN COOP SALAD

Feel cooped up? Invite that little cowgirl you met at the honky-tonk over for this light lunch. This just might be the time to throw Mickey Gilley's "Put Your Dreams Away" or Johnny Lee's "Bet Your Heart on Me" on the turntable. If she likes you, she just might invite *you* over for Luckenbach Peach Chicken (page 42).

  1 pound boned chicken, cooked and diced
 1/2 cup diced celery
 1/2 cup sweet relish
 1/4 teaspoon black pepper
 1/2 teaspoon salt
 1/8 teaspoon garlic salt
 1/2 cup Miracle Whip
 1/2 cup crushed pecans or almonds
  1 tablespoon parsley flakes
Lettuce or toast

1. In a large bowl mix thoroughly all ingredients except lettuce or toast. Chill.
2. Serve on lettuce cups or toast.

SERVES 2

EL GRANDE GUACAMOLE SALAD

You'll be coming back for more of this guacamole—the star of any Mexican dish.

6 to 8 avocados, peeled and diced
Juice of 2 lemons
  1 large tomato, diced
  1 teaspoon Tabasco sauce
¹/₈ teaspoon black pepper
¹/₄ teaspoon salt
¹/₈ teaspoon garlic salt
  1 small yellow onion, chopped
Shredded lettuce
Tortilla chips

1. In a large bowl, combine all ingredients except last 2 and mix thoroughly.
2. Serve on a bed of shredded lettuce and garnish with tortilla chips.

SERVES 4

VARIATION: *To make an avocado dip, add ¹/₂ cup Miracle Whip and blend with mixer until fairly smooth.*

BAYOU SHRIMP SALAD

A tasty, delightful dish that can turn any cowboy into a seafood lover. This is an easy dish to whip up on a lazy afternoon before you hit the honky-tonks.

2 pounds shrimp, boiled and chopped
1 medium head cabbage, shredded
1/2 cup grated carrots
1 cup blue cheese dressing
1/2 cup sweet relish
1/8 teaspoon black pepper
1/4 teaspoon salt
1 tablespoon sugar

Combine all ingredients in a bowl and mix thoroughly. Serve chilled.

SERVES 4 TO 6

TEARJERKER SALAD

This salad is so delicious that chances are you'll cry when it's all gone. But don't worry; it's so easy to make.

4 cucumbers, sliced
1 purple onion, sliced
2 green onions, diced
1 cup sliced fresh mushrooms
1 cup fresh cauliflower pieces
1 1/2 cups buttermilk salad dressing

Combine all ingredients in a large bowl and mix thoroughly. Chill.

SERVES 6 TO 8

BANDIT BEAN SALAD

This bean salad isn't called bandit for nothin'. It'll steal your heart, pardner.

1 16-ounce can kidney beans
1 8-ounce can whole-kernel corn
1 8-ounce can English peas
1 8-ounce can string beans
$1/2$ cup chopped white onions
$2/3$ cup Miracle Whip
$1/3$ cup sweet relish
$1/2$ teaspoon salt
$1/8$ teaspoon black pepper
2 tablespoons light Karo syrup or honey

After draining all excess juice from cans, combine all ingredients in a large bowl and blend thoroughly. Serve chilled.

SERVES 4 TO 6

PANHANDLE POTATO SALAD

Get a handle on this potato salad, and you'll never let go.

   4 *cups diced boiled potatoes*
   4 *eggs, hard-boiled and diced*
  $1/2$ *cup diced celery*
  $1/2$ *cup diced yellow onion*
  $1/2$ *cup sweet relish*
  $1/2$ *cup Miracle Whip*
   3 *teaspoons mustard*
  $1/2$ *teaspoon salt*
  $1/4$ *teaspoon black pepper*
Paprika
Parsley flakes

1. Combine all ingredients except last 2 in a large bowl and blend thoroughly. Chill.
2. Garnish with paprika and parsley flakes.

SERVES 4 TO 6

HOG-GREASE SPINACH SALAD

Even if you didn't like spinach as a kid, you'll go hog wild over this spinach dish.

  6 ounces smoked slab bacon, sliced into $1/4$-inch strips
$1/2$ teaspoon black pepper
$1/2$ teaspoon garlic salt
  1 pound fresh leaf spinach, washed, drained, and torn into
     bite-size pieces
  4 eggs, hard-boiled and diced
  4 green onions, chopped

1. In a skillet fry bacon with pepper and garlic salt until crisp.
2. Remove bacon and break into small pieces, and return to grease.
3. Place spinach in a large bowl. Add warm bacon and grease, eggs, and onions. Toss together and serve immediately.

SERVES 4

2

DOWN HOME SAVORY SAUCES

TEXAS LIGHTNING CHILI GRAVY

Pardner, this is it. The chili gravy to make all those Tex-Mex dishes Texas good.

  3 whole dried chile pods, seeds removed
  1 clove garlic
1 1/2 teaspoons ground comino
Salt to taste
  1 jalapeño pepper, seeds removed

1. Put some water in a saucepan and add chile pods; boil approximately 5 minutes.
2. Put boiled chiles and liquid from boiling in a blender with garlic, comino, salt, and jalapeño. Blend 1 minute.
3. Put mixture in a cast-iron skillet and cook over medium heat for 15 minutes, or until chili gravy thickens slightly.

YIELDS APPROXIMATELY 1/2 CUP

SPANISH SAUCE

A must for Tex-Mex dishes.

  6 large ripe tomatoes
  2 large onions, diced
  2 teaspoons vegetable oil
Salt and black pepper to taste

1. Grate fresh tomatoes on cheese grater and throw away skin.
2. Put onions and oil in a pot, add tomatoes, salt, and pepper.
3. Cook until onions are clear and tomatoes are done. If mixture gets too dry, add water and continue cooking.

YIELDS APPROXIMATELY 1 1/2 CUPS

GREEN ENCHILADA SAUCE

This easy-to-fix sauce is just what you need to make the Casa Grande Enchilada (page 46) *muy bueno.*

  1 *tablespoon vegetable oil*
  6 *tomatillos (small green tomatoes), chopped*
  1 *medium onion, chopped*
  1 *clove garlic, chopped*
  2 *medium jalapeño peppers, seeded and chopped*
1¹/₂ *teaspoons ground comino*
  2 *cups water (if sauce is too thick, add additional water)*

1. Heat oil in a skillet and sauté tomatillos, onion, and garlic until onion is clear.
2. Add jalapeños, comino, and water.
3. Simmer for approximately 15 to 20 minutes.

YIELDS APPROXIMATELY 2 CUPS

PICO DE GALLO

Designed to give Tex-Mex food that special flavor.

  2 *fresh tomatoes*
  1 *medium white onion*
  3 *jalapeño peppers, seeds removed*
 ¹/₂ *bunch cilantro*

Chop all ingredients and mix well. Store in a jar in the refrigerator.

YIELDS 2 CUPS

BARBED WIRE BARBECUE SAUCE

For a barbecue sauce with real bite, try this on your dish. What a way to wake up the flavor. It's a barbecue lover's dream.

4 ounces (1 stick) butter
1 onion, chopped
2 cloves garlic, chopped
4 tablespoons Worcestershire sauce
Juice of 2 lemons
1/2 teaspoon black pepper
1 tablespoon salt
2 tablespoons paprika
1 8-ounce can tomato sauce
1 whole tomato, diced
2 cups tomato catsup
1 12-ounce can beer

1. Melt butter in large pot at medium heat.
2. Add onion, garlic, Worcestershire sauce, lemon juice, black pepper, salt, and paprika.
3. Cook and stir constantly until onion is soft.
4. Stir in remaining ingredients. Simmer at low heat for 1 hour. If sauce becomes too thick, add water to desired consistency.

YIELDS APPROXIMATELY 2 QUARTS (8 CUPS)

BUCKAROO BARBECUE SAUCE

This sauce puts the spirit of Texas into every bite.

$1/4$ cup butter
$1/2$ onion, chopped
$1/4$ cup vinegar
$1/4$ cup catsup
$1/4$ cup lemon juice
$1/4$ cup Worcestershire sauce
 1 teaspoon salt
$1/4$ teaspoon garlic powder

1. Melt butter in a saucepan and sauté onions.
2. Add all other ingredients and bring to a slow boil.
3. Reduce heat and simmer for about 20 minutes. Serve warm.

YIELDS APPROXIMATELY 1 CUP

SIX-SHOOTER CREAM SAUCE

Shoot your favorite dish with this cream sauce. You'll be right on target.

 3 tablespoons butter
 3 tablespoons flour
 2 cups milk
 1 teaspoon salt
$1/8$ teaspoon black pepper

1. Melt butter in a saucepan over low heat.
2. Blend in flour and milk, stirring constantly.
3. Add seasonings and cook until thick and smooth.

YIELDS 2 CUPS

WAGON WHEEL BATTER

Roll your chicken or shrimp in this batter, and you're on the trail to some good eatin'.

   1 egg
 3/4 cup milk
   1 cup flour
   1 teaspoon salt
 1/8 teaspoon black pepper

1. In a bowl beat egg lightly with a fork. Stir in milk, flour, and seasonings.
2. To serve, dip food into batter, and let excess batter drain off. In a skillet of hot oil (375°), place one piece at a time, frying to a golden brown.

YIELDS APPROXIMATELY 1 1/4 CUPS

SWEET IRON STEAK BASTE

The best baste for bringing out the taste of Texas in steaks.

1/2 cup vegetable oil
 1 small yellow onion, chopped
 1 tablespoon salt
 1 tablespoon black pepper
 1 teaspoon garlic salt
1/2 cup Worcestershire sauce
 4 tablespoons parsley flakes
 1 12-ounce can beer, room temperature
 1 12-ounce can Coca-Cola, room temperature

1. In a large saucepan heat oil and sauté onions and seasonings at medium heat until onions are soft (about 8 minutes).
2. Slowly add beer and Coke, increase heat, and bring to a boil for 3 minutes.
3. Reduce heat and keep warm.
4. To serve, dip steaks in baste before cooking over hardwood charcoal fire. Spoon baste over steaks each time they are turned, and cook to taste (rare, medium, well, etc.).

YIELDS APPROXIMATELY 3 CUPS

SHRIMP BOAT SAUCE

Set your sails for this scrumptious seafood sauce. Serve with fried fish or as a stuffing for crabs or fish.

1/4 cup margarine
1 cup diced boiled shrimp
1 cup diced boiled crab meat
4 green onions, diced
1 teaspoon gumbo filé
1 teaspoon garlic salt
1/2 teaspoon red (cayenne) pepper
1/4 cup Worcestershire sauce
1 12-ounce can beer
4 cups crumbled Corral Corn Bread (page 130) or store-bought

1. Preheat oven to 350°.
2. In a 2-quart casserole or Dutch oven heat margarine and sauté shrimp, crab, onion, and seasonings over medium heat for 5 minutes.
3. Add beer, stir in corn bread.
4. Bake, uncovered, for 20 minutes or until fairly dry.

SERVES 4 TO 6

DOUGHBELLY DRESSING

Just the right stuff—or stuffing—for your favorite chicken or turkey.

2 cups water
1 pound chicken giblets, diced
1/2 yellow onion, chopped
1 cup diced celery
1 tablespoon salt
1/2 teaspoon black pepper
1/8 teaspoon garlic salt
4 cups crumbled Corral Corn Bread (page 130) or store-bought

1. Preheat oven to 350°.
2. In a 2-quart casserole or Dutch oven add water and boil giblets, onion, celery, and seasonings until giblets are tender.
3. Stir in corn bread.
4. Bake, uncovered, for 20 minutes or until fairly dry.

SERVES 4 TO 6

SEAFOOD DIP

This makes a great dipping sauce for any seafood.

  1 cup Miracle Whip
  4 green onions, diced
  3 eggs, hard-boiled and finely diced
1 1/2 tablespoons hot mustard
Juice of 2 lemons
  1 teaspoon garlic salt
1/8 teaspoon black pepper

Combine all ingredients in a bowl and chill at least 2 hours before using.

YIELDS APPROXIMATELY 1 1/2 CUPS

BOOTJACK BROCCOLI DIP

You'll get a boot out of this fancy dip. Ideal for those times when you just want to snack.

¹/₂ cup margarine
 4 green onions, chopped
 1 tablespoon flour
¹/₂ teaspoon garlic powder
 1 stalk broccoli, finely chopped
 2 cups grated longhorn cheddar cheese
 1 8-ounce can chopped mushrooms
 1 can cream of mushroom soup
 1 cup chopped almonds

1. In a skillet melt margarine and sauté onions, flour, and garlic powder over medium heat for 5 minutes.
2. Stir in broccoli, cheese, and mushrooms until cheese is melted.
3. Stir in mushroom soup.
4. Add almonds just before serving; serve warm.

YIELDS APPROXIMATELY 3 CUPS

3

STAMPEDE STOPPIN' ENTRÉES

A Few Words on Texas-Style Barbecue from Pat Wright

To say that the method of cooking meat with smoke and heat from a wood fire (better known as barbecue) is a Texas invention would be as untrue as saying that Texans discovered fire. Soon after discovering fire, ancient man found that in drying meat for future consumption, if he placed the meat near a fire, the smoke and heat from the fire would keep insects and predators away from the meat and would also speed up the drying process. The aroma and flavor that the meat picked up from the fire so pleased him that he started moving the meat closer and closer to the fire; soon the meat was actually being cooked by the fire. He soon discovered that the cooked meat was tender and easier to eat. Thus, through the ages, man has continued to enjoy this method of cooking meat.

Texas, because of it's vast amount of range land, was ideally suited for the cattle industry. Cattlemen often had to move their herds from one grazing range to another, and also had to drive them long distances to market. Because of this, they often had to live and work outdoors, often at a different location each day. Therefore, they were forced to cook over a campfire. But don't think barbecued beef was on the menu everyday; it was mostly beans and hard-tack biscuits. If for one reason or another a steer or cow had to be butchered, it was a special treat to have a little beef on your tin plate. If at all possible, the meat was sold or traded for more beans, flour, salt, and coffee because these foods would keep better and go a lot further. So a tradition was begun, and Texans—the type of people who hold to tradition as something very special—consider a barbecue a special event no matter what the occasion, if any.

Texans enjoy barbecue so much that they have refined and developed it to a fine art known as "Texas-Style Barbecue." This is broken into two methods; the cut of meat you are going to barbecue determines the method. Large cuts of beef, pork, mutton, or goat roasts, whole chickens and turkeys, and whole slabs of ribs are cooked in what is known as a barbecue pit. The barbecue pit can also be used to slow-smoke sausage links, fish, and many types of wild game. Smaller, more tender cuts of beef and pork—such as steaks and chops, cut-up chicken and turkey, small or cut-up slabs of ribs, hamburger meat, precooked or smoked links, franks, fish, and small wild game—can be cooked on what is known as a barbecue grill.

Barbecue pits come in hundreds of different shapes, sizes, and styles. They are made from either brick or metal or both. They range from the small backyard pits, which will cook for a dozen or so people, to the large commercial pits like the one at Gilley's Club, which cooks thirteen hundred pounds of beef at one time.

Although there are many different types of barbecue pits, they all function in the same way. The meat is cooked by indirect heat and smoke from the wood fire—the meat is never placed directly over the fire. At one end of the pit is a door that opens into the fire box and is used for loading the wood and cleaning out the ashes. The air intake, which consists of adjustable vents that control the amount of air fed to the fire, is usually on this door. At the other end of the pit is an exhaust (smokestack) with an adjustable flue to control the amount of heat and smoke that is released from the pit. The intake and exhaust control the draft or air flow to the fire. The more they are opened up, the greater the draft, in this way feeding the fire more air and increasing the heat of the fire.

Some pits require large logs that must burn for up to twelve to fourteen hours, but they are just for longevity; the heat is still controlled by the draft. The fire is at one end of the pit and the meat is placed on a grill or rack at the other end of the pit. The grill or rack is at least six inches above the level of the fire so that the heat and smoke can pass over and under the meat. Cooking time is determined by many factors—type, size, and cut of meat; size of fire; control of draft; desired tenderness. One thing that usually holds true with all meat is the need for a constant cooking temperature of 250°. At this temperature, about one hour cooking time is required for every pound of beef. Some pits are designed to be used as both a pit and a grill, which is ideal for the backyard. This type of pit is built with the fire grate across the entire bottom of the pit so it can be used as a grill for steaks, franks, etcetera.

The four most popular types of wood to use in barbecue pits are hickory, pecan, mesquite, and all types of oak. Soft woods such as pine, cottonwood, willow, and tallow trees burn too fast and leave a bitter taste on the meat.

Natural gas or propane is, of course, the easiest way to start a fire, and the meat can already be on the pit. You can also use a small amount of hardwood charcoal or charcoal lighter fluid to start the wood, but make sure all the lighter fluid is burned off before placing the meat on the pit so that the meat will not pick up the gas taste from the lighter fluid.

Barbecue grills are sold commercially everywhere and come in all kinds of shapes, sizes, and price ranges. Some are even big enough and designed in a way to be used as a pit. Most barbecue grills are designed to use charcoal; there are many brands, but the best is pure hardwood charcoal. Hickory, pecan, mesquite, and oak chips or kindling are also sold commercially and do add a great deal of flavor to meat. There is also a little-known secret I will share with you: Whenever you get a chance to pick up green pecans that have been blown down, grab up as many as you can, and freeze them in freezer bags. The next time you are going to barbecue on your grill, throw a handful of the green pecans right on top of the hot coals. When the pecans begin to smoke real good, slap those steaks, chickens, or burgers on the grill. All the folks will wonder what you do to make your meat taste so great. Maybe you'll tell them, and maybe you won't.

Again, natural gas or propane is the best to start charcoal, but liquid fuel lighter is the most common and convenient. Use only charcoal lighter fluid, because it is designed to start slow and burn slow. Never use gasoline or other liquid fuels because they have a very high flash point and are very dangerous. The amount of charcoal to be used is determined by how hot a fire you want and how long you want the fire to burn. (Small or tender cuts of meat generally can be cooked hot and fast. Larger or tougher cuts of meat need to cook at a lower temperature and longer.) When applying the lighter fluid, cover all the charcoal completely, let it soak about a minute, then light. Make sure your air intake is open all the way, and don't cover the grill or you may smother the fire. When the lighter fluid has all burned off and the charcoal has taken on a gray color, the charcoal is then producing an even heat which can be controlled by the air intake. Less air—less heat; more air—more heat.

If you are going to apply barbecue sauce to the meat while it is still on the grill, wait till the last few minutes of cooking.

I hope this will help everyone to understand Texas-Style Barbecue a little better, but if it doesn't, just come on down to Gilley's and let us show you.

One last note, the Texas way to spell Barbecue is Bar-B-Que.

BEER FRIED FISH

What a way to kick off an evening with Beer Fried Fish. But be sure and leave some of the beer for the fish.

1– 2 pounds fish fillets, or about 6 small pan fish
12 ounces beer
1 cup flour
1/2 cup yellow cornmeal
1 tablespoon salt
1/2 teaspoon black pepper
4 cups hot vegetable oil

1. Place fish in bowl, pour in beer, and mix around to make sure fish are covered with beer. Let marinate in refrigerator about 2 hours.
2. Remove fish and save beer.
3. Combine flour, cornmeal, salt, and pepper in plate.
4. Roll fish in flour mix to coat. Shake off excess. Dip in beer, and let excess drain off. Then coat again with flour mix.
5. Drop individual fillets into hot oil (about 375° F., medium heat), and deep fry until golden brown.

SERVES 2 TO 4

SAN JACINTO SHRIMP

This is a fun and tasty way to fix shrimp.

24 jumbo shrimp, tails left on
 1 small can button mushroom caps
 8 cherry tomatoes
 4 pearl onions
 4 large stuffed green olives
 4 stainless steel skewers, 10 inches long and about $1/8$ inch
    diameter
Sweet Iron Steak Baste (page 29) or Barbed Wire Barbecue
Sauce (page 26)

1. Stick ingredients on skewers in this order: shrimp, mushroom cap, tomato, shrimp, pearl onion, shrimp, mushroom cap, shrimp, tomato, shrimp, and an olive.
2. Cook over hardwood charcoal fire until shrimp are light brown. Shrimp should be turned to each side at least twice while cooking. Baste with Sweet Iron Steak Baste every 10 to 15 seconds, or wait until shrimp just starts to turn pink and baste with Barbed Wire Barbecue Sauce until shrimp are done.

SERVES 4

SERVING SUGGESTION: Serve on bed of Ranch Rice with Hog-tied Spinach and Not-So-Quiet Hush Puppies.

LUCKENBACH PEACH CHICKEN

You'll keep lookin' back for more of this zesty dish. What a peachy way to prepare a chicken.

 4 chicken breasts
1/8 teaspoon black pepper
1/4 teaspoon salt
1/2 teaspoon cinnamon
 1 16-ounce can peach halves in heavy syrup

1. Preheat oven to 350°.
2. Place chicken breasts in 2-inch-deep casserole pan and dust with seasonings.
3. Bake for 10 minutes.
4. Pour half of peach syrup over chicken. Bake for another 10 minutes.
5. Place remainder of syrup and peach halves around chicken. Bake 10 to 15 minutes, or until glazed brown.

SERVES 4

SERVING SUGGESTION: Best with fresh steamed garden vegetables.

CHICKEN RANCH DELIGHT

This barbecued chicken dish will put a smile on any cowboy's face.

  8 ounces *Texas Lightning Chili Gravy (page 24)*
  1 *large cut-up fryer*
Juice of 1 lemon
  $1/4$ *cup chili powder*
  $1/4$ *teaspoon black pepper*
  $1/8$ *teaspoon garlic salt*
  $1/2$ *teaspoon salt*
  $1/8$ *teaspoon celery salt*

1. In a small saucepan heat chili gravy.
2. Brush on and completely cover the chicken with lemon juice.
3. Combine all seasonings.
4. Apply seasonings to chicken, completely covering it.
5. Cook chicken over hardwood charcoal fire until completely tender.
6. Place chicken in large serving dish, and pour chili gravy over chicken.

SERVES 4

SERVING SUGGESTION: Serve with roasted corn on the cob or Spanish Rice (page 125).

BRONCO BROILED CHICKEN

You'll flip for this barbecued chicken—the best!

      8 ounces (2 sticks) butter
      4 green onions, chopped
Juice of 4 lemons
      1/4 cup Worcestershire sauce
      1/8 teaspoon garlic powder
      1/2 teaspoon salt
      1/4 teaspoon black pepper
      1/8 teaspoon paprika
      1/4 teaspoon parsley flakes
      1/8 teaspoon celery salt
      1 large cut-up chicken

1. In a skillet melt butter and sauté onions.
2. Add lemon juice and seasonings, and simmer over medium heat for about 10 to 12 minutes.
3. Dip chicken into lemon butter before putting on grill.
4. Cook chicken over hardwood charcoal fire, basting and turning every 6 to 8 minutes for approximately 20 to 30 minutes, depending on size of chicken, heat, and fire.

SERVES 4

SERVING SUGGESTION: Serve with roasted corn on the cob, Ranch Rice (page 123), or baked potato.

STOVE-TOP BARBECUE CHICKEN

Now you can have that Texas barbecue flavor in your own kitchen. Substitute 2–3 pounds beef or pork, cut into 1-inch strips, if you want a heartier meat.

2 cups water
3 cups Barbed Wire Barbecue Sauce (page 26)
2 young chickens, cut up

1. In large pot add water to barbecue sauce and bring to slow boil.
2. Add chicken and simmer at low heat, covered, for about 1 hour or until chicken is tender.

SERVES 4 TO 6

CASA GRANDE ENCHILADA

This Tex-Mex dish is made with chicken, cheese, and sour cream, and is much more than just an enchilada.

 1 *whole chicken*
Salt and pepper to taste
 1 *cup vegetable oil*
12 *tortillas*
¹/₂ pint sour cream
 1 *recipe Green Enchilada Sauce (page 25)*
 4 *ounces cheddar cheese, grated*

1. In a pot of water boil chicken. When cooked, season with salt and pepper, remove meat from bones, and shred chicken meat.
2. Heat oil in a skillet; dip each tortilla in hot oil and place them on a platter.
3. Preheat oven to 350°.
4. Put chicken on each tortilla slightly off center with 1 teaspoon sour cream.
5. Roll tortillas and place in a layer in a casserole dish.
6. Cover with green sauce and top with grated cheese.
7. Bake for approximately 10 minutes.

SERVES 4

CHICKEN ON THE NEST

Here that chicken flavor really comes alive.

1/4 cup margarine
1 yellow onion, diced
1 large cut-up fryer
1/4 cup Worcestershire sauce
1 tablespoon salt
1 teaspoon black pepper
1/2 teaspoon celery salt
2 bay leaves
1/2 teaspoon celery salt
4 cups water
1 can cream of mushroom soup
2 cups uncooked long-grain rice

1. In a deep skillet heat margarine and sauté onions, chicken, and seasonings over medium heat for 10 minutes. Stir often.
2. Increase heat to high, add water, stir in mushroom soup, and bring to a boil.
3. Reduce heat, cover, and simmer until chicken is tender.
4. Increase heat to high, stir in rice, and bring to a boil.
5. Reduce heat, cover, and simmer until rice is tender and water is absorbed. (Don't uncover or stir the first 15 minutes after adding rice.)

SERVES 6 TO 8

RIO ROAST CHICKEN

You'll never want to roast a chicken any other way after the Rio way.

 2 medium-size chickens
¹/₂ cup margarine, melted
 1 cup cranberry sauce
¹/₂ cup apple cider
 3 tablespoons honey
 2 tablespoons orange juice
 2 teaspoons cornstarch
¹/₂ teaspoon salt

1. Roast chickens in pan at 370°F. for 1 hour and 15 minutes, basting frequently with margarine.
2. In saucepan combine cranberry sauce, cider, honey, orange juice, cornstarch, and salt, with any margarine left in roasting pan.
3. Simmer on low heat for 15 minutes.
4. Brush sauce over chicken for last 15 minutes of roasting.

SERVES 4 TO 6

TRINITY BAY GUMBO

You don't have to live on Trinity Bay to make this gumbo; just follow the Trinity Bay recipe to make a huge batch. Invite the gang or freeze for another hungry day.

1/4 cup vegetable oil
  1 large onion, diced
  1 large bell pepper, seeded and diced
  1 cup diced celery
  2 cloves garlic, finely chopped
  2 teaspoons salt
  1 teaspoon black pepper
  2 bay leaves
1/4 cup Worcestershire sauce
1/4 teaspoon red (cayenne) pepper
  2 tablespoons gumbo filé
  4 tablespoons flour
  1 pint oysters
  1 pound medium shelled shrimp
  1 pound lump crab meat
  1 pound fish fillets (any edible saltwater fish)
  1 can beef bouillon soup
  8 cups hot water

1. In a large stockpot heat oil and sauté onion, bell pepper, celery, garlic, and seasonings over medium heat for 5 minutes.
2. Add flour and brown dark, stirring constantly.
3. Add oysters, shrimp, crab, and fish, and sauté for 5 minutes.
4. Add bouillon and water, stirring thoroughly. Increase heat and bring to a boil.
5. Reduce to low heat and simmer for 30 minutes.

YIELDS 5 TO 6 QUARTS

SERVING SUGGESTION: *Serve over long-grain or brown rice.*

SHRIMP AND OKRA STEW

This is stew-licious. A whole new taste to shrimp—and to okra.

1 16-ounce can stewed okra
1 16-ounce can stewed tomatoes
1 bay leaf
4 peppercorns
1 cup water
1½ teaspoons salt
2 pounds shelled shrimp
½ teaspoon gumbo filé

1. Combine all ingredients except shrimp and filé in a large pot and bring to a boil.
2. Reduce heat and simmer for about 15 minutes.
3. Add shrimp and filé and simmer for about 15 minutes more.

SERVES 4 TO 6

SERVING SUGGESTION: *This stew is best over a bed of long-grain or enriched rice.*

LONE STAR STEW

If you don't find it in Lone Star Stew, then it ain't worth eatin'.

2 pounds beef tips cut into 1 1/2" to 2" cubes
1 cup plus 3 tablespoons flour
1/4 cup margarine
1 yellow onion, diced
2 teaspoons salt
1 teaspoon black pepper
1/2 teaspoon red (cayenne) pepper
1 clove garlic, diced
1 bell pepper, seeded and diced
2 bay leaves
1/4 cup Worcestershire sauce
8 cups water
1 cup diced celery
4 medium-size potatoes, peeled and sliced
6 carrots, peeled and sliced

1. Roll beef in 1 cup flour.
2. In a deep skillet or Dutch oven melt margarine and sauté onion, beef, salt and peppers, garlic, bell pepper, bay leaves, and Worcestershire sauce at low heat for about 10 minutes.
3. Stir in 3 tablespoons flour and brown lightly.
4. Stir in water and slowly bring to boil.
5. Reduce heat and simmer, covered, for 30 to 40 minutes, until meat is fairly tender.
6. Add celery, potatoes, and carrots and return to a boil.
7. Reduce heat and simmer again, covered, until vegetables are tender.

SERVES 6 TO 8

SERVING SUGGESTION: *Serve with corn bread—store-bought or Corral Corn Bread (page 130).*

GILLEY'S CHILI CON CARNE

You'll be singing the praises of this chili, just like Mickey himself. Just spicy enough to make any cook an "overnight sensation."

   4 chile pods, seeds removed
   4 cups water
  1/4 cup margarine
   1 cup chopped onions
   2 teaspoons comino seed
  1/4 cup chili powder
  1/2 tablespoon black pepper
   2 cloves garlic, chopped
   2 tablespoons salt
   2 pounds lean ground beef (or venison or rabbit)
   3 tablespoons flour

1. In a saucepan, simmer chile pods in 4 cups of water until pods become soft.
2. In a large stockpot, melt margarine over medium heat and add onions and seasonings; simmer until onions are soft.
3. Add ground beef and flour, and cook until completely brown, stirring occasionally.
4. Add water and chile pods. Cover and simmer over low heat for 30 to 45 minutes.

YIELDS APPROXIMATELY 2 QUARTS

CHILES RELLENOS

Once you try this favorite Tex-Mex dish, you'll want to say *"Olé!"*

6 *whole* chiles poblanos *or bell peppers*
1 *tablespoon vegetable oil*
1 *medium potato, diced*
1 *medium white onion, diced*
1 *clove garlic*
1 *pound lean ground beef*
1 *teaspoon salt*
1/2 *teaspoon black pepper*
1 *teaspoon ground comino*
4 *whole eggs*
1 *cup flour*
4 *ounces cheddar cheese, grated*
3 *cups heated Spanish Sauce (page 24)*

1. Roast chiles on hot griddle until well-toasted. Set aside to cool.
2. In large cast-iron skillet heat oil and fry potatoes; add onions and garlic.
3. Cook slightly, and add ground beef, salt, pepper, and comino. Cook until done.
4. Skin roasted peppers, make a slit in them, and remove seeds. (Seeds will be very hot.)
5. Stuff peppers with ground beef and potato mixture. Close with toothpicks.
6. Separate yolks from white of eggs, and in a bowl beat whites until firm as meringue.
7. Add egg yolks to whites and mix well.
8. Roll stuffed peppers in flour and dip in egg batter.
9. Fry peppers until batter is golden brown.
10. Top with grated cheese and Spanish Sauce.

SERVES 6

NOTE: Chiles Rellenos can be made ahead and refrigerated, then heated with cheese and Spanish Sauce.

SERVING SUGGESTION: Best accompanied by Refried Beans (page 126) and Spanish Rice (page 125).

EL TORO TACO

Riding El Toro, the mechanical bull, just might make you mighty hungry. To satisfy that hunger, why not grab an El Toro Taco, and wash it down with Gilley's Beer.

$1/2$ cup vegetable oil
$1/2$ medium onion, chopped
1 clove garlic
1 jalapeño pepper, seeds removed (optional)
1 pound lean ground beef
Salt
$1 1/2$ teaspoons ground comino
1 teaspoon chili powder
12 taco shells
1 head lettuce, chopped
2 ripe tomatoes, diced
4 ounces cheddar cheese, grated

1. In a skillet heat 1 tablespoon oil and sauté onions, garlic, and jalapeño until onions are clear.
2. Add ground beef, and cook until almost done.
3. Add salt, comino, and chili powder.
4. In a skillet or fryer heat about $1/2$ inch of oil and fry taco shells on each side. Fold in half and fry each side till nearly crisp. Set aside and drain.
5. Place a tablespoon of meat mixture in taco shell, stuff with lettuce and tomatoes, and top with cheese.

SERVES 4

ENVUELTOS DE PICADILLO

This Tex-Mex dish means an envelope of chopped seasoned beef. And it also means you're in for some good-tasting food.

1/2 cup vegetable oil
1 medium white onion, diced
2 cloves garlic
1 jalapeño pepper, seeded and chopped (optional)
1 pound lean ground beef
1 teaspoon salt
1/2 teaspoon black pepper
1 heaping tablespoon ground comino
1/2 teaspoon chili powder
12 tortillas
6 cups Spanish Sauce (page 24)
1/2 pound mild cheddar or American cheese, grated

1. In a skillet heat 1 tablespoon oil and sauté onions, garlic, and jalapeño over medium heat.
2. Add ground beef and brown slightly.
3. Add salt, pepper, comino, and chili powder and cook over medium heat until done (approximately 15 minutes).
4. Preheat oven to 350°.
5. In a skillet heat remaining oil and dip tortillas, one at a time, in hot oil to soften. Fry till nearly crisp.
6. In a casserole dish place a tablespoon of meat mixture in tortilla and roll up. Cover with Spanish Sauce and grated cheese.
7. Place in oven until hot and cheese is melted.

SERVES 4

BEEF ENCHILADAS

These flavorful beef enchiladas will make a good neighbor to the Cheese Enchiladas (page 71) on your plate.

  1 *cup vegetable oil*
  1 *medium onion, chopped*
  1 *clove garlic*
  1 *pound lean ground beef*
1 1/2 *teaspoons ground comino*
  1 *teaspoon chili powder*
Salt to taste
12 *corn tortillas*
  2 *cups Texas Lightning Chili Gravy (page 24)*
1/2 *cup grated cheddar cheese*

1. In a skillet heat 1 tablespoon oil and sauté half the onions and garlic clove until onions are clear.
2. Add ground beef and cook until almost done.
3. Add comino, chili powder, and salt, and finish cooking.
4. Heat remaining oil in a skillet and dip folded corn tortilla in hot oil with tongs till almost crisp.
5. Preheat oven to 350°.
6. Place tortilla in hot chili gravy for approximately 1/2 minute, then place on flat baking sheet.
7. Put 1 tablespoon of beef mixture slightly off center of tortilla and roll up. Repeat for all tortillas.
8. Pour remaining chili gravy over enchiladas and top with grated cheese and remaining onions.
9. Place in oven for 15 minutes.

SERVES 4

SERVING SUGGESTION: Try with Refried Beans (page 126) and Ranch Rice (page 123).

FIESTA TAMALE PIE

Anytime you taste this tamale pie, it's cause for a fiesta. It's easy to fix, and easy to get hooked on.

4 corn tortillas, halved lengthwise
1 pound lean ground beef
1 16-ounce can whole-kernel corn, drained
2/3 cup sliced ripe olives
1 16-ounce can tomato sauce
1 cup grated cheddar cheese

1. Preheat oven to 375°.
2. Place tortilla halves in a 2-quart casserole dish and set aside.
3. Brown ground beef in a skillet and drain off grease.
4. Spread beef over tortillas.
5. Spread on corn, olives, tomato sauce, and cheese.
6. Bake, uncovered, for 30 to 45 minutes.

SERVES 4 TO 6

POKER CHIP PIE

There's no gamble when you try this dish: You'll be the winner.

> 1 *large bag Fritos corn or tortilla chips*
> 2 *cups Gilley's Chili con Carne (page 52), homemade, or canned chili*
> 1 *large yellow onion, diced*
> 2 *cups grated cheddar cheese*

1. Preheat oven to 325°F.
2. In a large casserole dish, place thin layer of chips.
3. Cover with chili.
4. Sprinkle with onion and cheese.
5. Repeat layers until all ingredients are used.
6. Cover and place in oven for approximately 30 minutes.
7. Uncover and cook for 5 more minutes. Serve.

SERVES 4

SERVING SUGGESTION: Pie goes best with steaming hot Spanish Rice (page 125)—canned or homemade. Or try Ranch Rice (page 123).

PIG RUSTLER'S SPECIAL

Don't be caught rustlin' this grub off of your neighbor's plate, pardner.

  1 cup flour
  1 teaspoon baking powder
  4 center-cut pork chops, 3/4 to 1 inch thick
 1/2 cup vegetable oil
  1 yellow onion, diced
 1/2 teaspoon salt
 1/8 teaspoon black pepper
  1 cup milk
  1 8-ounce can sliced mushrooms

1. Mix flour and baking powder and roll pork chops in mixture.
2. Place in a 10-inch skillet with hot oil and cook over medium heat until light brown. Remove pork chops and set aside.
3. Add onions, salt, pepper, and 4 tablespoons flour mixture, and brown lightly. Stir constantly.
4. Add milk and stir until creamy smooth for about 6 to 8 minutes. (If too thick, add water.)
5. Return chops to skillet and add mushrooms.
6. Cover and let simmer over low heat for about 20 minutes, or until pork chops are tender.

SERVES 2 TO 4

CATTLE RUSTLER'S SPECIAL

Follow the same recipe as pig rustler's special, but use either round steak, beef tips, flank steak, or fajitas (beef skirt steak).

PICKETT'S BAYOU PORK

This is the way that pork was meant to be cooked—the Pickett's Bayou way.

    2 tablespoons margarine
  1/2 cup chopped green onion
    1 clove garlic, chopped
    3 tablespoons dried parsley flakes
  1/2 teaspoon thyme
    1 bay leaf
  1/4 teaspoon cayenne pepper
    2 cups beef broth
    1 pound fresh pork, diced and seasoned with salt and pepper

1. Heat margarine and sauté onions and seasonings until soft.
2. Add broth and pork, and bring to low boil.
3. Reduce heat to low, and simmer about 30 minutes or until pork is tender.

SERVES 4 TO 6

SERVING SUGGESTION: Serve with Ranch Rice (page 123) and green vegetables.

BARBAROSA BAKED HAM

This is ham good!!!

4 tablespoons wine vinegar
1 teaspoon marjoram
1 teaspoon oregano
1 teaspoon thyme
1 teaspoon salt
1/2 teaspoon red pepper
1 5-pound cured ham, bone in
2 6-ounce cans unsweetened orange juice

1. Preheat oven to 350°.
2. In small bowl combine vinegar and dry spices, and stir well.
3. Cover ham on all sides with spice paste.
4. Place ham in oven, and bake for about 1 1/2 hours.
5. Pour orange juice over ham, and bake for about 30 minutes more, basting frequently.

SERVES 4 TO 6

RAINY DAY BARBECUE

Of course this is ideal for those sunny days, too.

Margarine
  2 *young chickens, cut-up, or 2–3 pounds beef or pork, cut
      into 1-inch-thick strips*
  3 *cups Barbed Wire Barbecue Sauce (page 26)*

1. Preheat oven to 375°.
2. Coat shallow baking pan with margarine.
3. Arrange meat in single layer in pan.
4. Spoon sauce over meat until well coated.
5. Bake in oven for 1 hour or until meat is tender (pork must be
    well done).
6. Serve with warm sauce on the side.

SERVES 4 TO 6

BEER POT ROAST

This dish is for the "real cowboy" who likes his beer and roast together. This will definitely get him in the honky-tonk spirit, and he just might be inclined to two-step to his pickup.

1/2 cup margarine
  1 onion, chopped
1/4 teaspoon black pepper
1/2 teaspoon salt
  2 cloves garlic, diced
  4 tablespoons Worcestershire sauce
1/8 teaspoon celery salt
  1 2- to 3-pound chuck roast
  1 12-ounce can beer
  4 ounces Coca-Cola
  1 16-ounce can whole peeled new potatoes
  1 16-ounce can baby carrots

1. Melt margarine in a 5- to 8-quart heavy pot over medium heat.
2. Add onion and seasonings. Sauté until onions are soft.
3. Place roast in pot and brown lightly on both sides.
4. Increase heat to high, add beer and Coke, and bring to a boil.
5. Reduce heat and simmer 30 minutes for each pound of meat.
6. Add potatoes and carrots. Cook for approximately 15 minutes over medium heat.

SERVES 4 TO 6

PASADENA PEPPER STEAK

You know this one has to be good if it's called "Pasadena." That's the home of the world's largest and best honky-tonk—Gilley's.

2 pounds round steak
1/2 cup flour
1/2 cup vegetable oil
1 yellow onion, sliced
1 cup sliced fresh mushrooms
1/4 teaspoon black pepper
1/2 teaspoon salt
1 clove garlic, chopped
4 teaspoons Worcestershire sauce
1 large bell pepper, seeded and sliced
1 cup water

1. Cut round steak into strips about 2 to 3 inches long and 1 inch wide, then roll strips in flour.
2. Heat oil in a skillet and add strips. Brown lightly over medium heat.
3. Add onions, mushrooms, and seasonings; cook for 5 minutes.
4. Add bell pepper and 2 teaspoons flour, cook for 5 more minutes.
5. Add water and stir; cover with lid and simmer over low heat for about 25 minutes or until meat is tender.

SERVES 4 TO 6

IRON SKILLET LIVER AND ONIONS

After this dinner, a cowboy can ride the mechanical bull all night long and pack a mean wallop on the punching bag.

 1 cup flour
 1/4 tablespoon baking powder
 4 tablespoons salt
 1/4 tablespoon black pepper
 1/8 teaspoon garlic salt
 1 tablespoon parsley flakes
 1 pound thin-sliced beef liver
 1/2 cup vegetable oil
 1 yellow onion, thin sliced
 1 cup milk

1. Combine flour, baking powder, and seasonings in a bowl.
2. Dredge liver in mixture until completely covered.
3. In a skillet heat oil and brown liver lightly on both sides. Remove liver and set aside.
4. Add onions and sauté until soft.
5. Add 4 tablespoons flour mixture and brown lightly over medium heat, stirring constantly.
6. Add milk and stir until creamy smooth (if too thick, add water).
7. Return liver and simmer over low heat about 20 to 30 minutes, or until liver is tender.

SERVES 2 TO 4

SERVING SUGGESTION: Serve with Ranch Rice (page 123) or green vegetables.

TEXAS TENDER MEAT LOAF

A real heart-melter.

2 pounds lean ground beef
1 cup bread crumbs or crumbled dried toast
1 small yellow onion, diced
1 bell pepper, seeded and diced
1/4 cup Worcestershire sauce
1/2 teaspoon garlic salt
1/4 teaspoon salt
1/2 teaspoon black pepper
1 8-ounce can stewed tomatoes (preferably Ro-tel)
1 8-ounce can tomato sauce (preferably Ro-tel)

1. Preheat oven to 350°.
2. In a large bowl, combine all ingredients except tomato sauce. Mold into loaf shape.
3. Place loaf in a 4-inch deep casserole dish and bake for 45 minutes.
4. Pour tomato sauce over loaf and bake 5 to 10 minutes more.

SERVES 6

BLACKJACK BEEF

This is beef enough for any cowboy or cowgirl, especially with that shot of whiskey.

2 pounds beef tips, cut into 1-inch cubes
1 small yellow onion, diced
1 cup sliced fresh mushrooms
1 teaspoon salt
$1/2$ teaspoon black pepper
1 teaspoon garlic salt
1 tablespoon parsley flakes
4 tablespoons Worcestershire sauce
1 can beef bouillon soup
6 ounces whiskey (preferably Jack Daniel's)

Combine all ingredients in a large heavy skillet or pan and cook, covered, over low heat for 2 to 3 hours, until meat is tender.

SERVES 4 TO 6

SERVING SUGGESTION: Serve over Ranch Rice (page 123).

AGUJAS

This is a very simple dish to make, and is ideal even for the noncook. If you can rub garlic on beef, you've got it.

1 clove garlic
3 pounds meaty short ribs of beef
Salt and black pepper to taste

1. Rub garlic over short ribs of beef and sprinkle liberally with salt and pepper.
2. Cook over charcoal for 8 minutes on one side and 5 minutes on the other side.

SERVES 6

SERVING SUGGESTION: Serve with Refried Beans (page 126), Spanish Rice (page 125), and Pico de Gallo (page 25).

TEXAS FAJITAS I

For a little south-of-the-border flavor, try this dish. It might turn you into an "urban vaquero."

  1 16-ounce bottle Italian dressing
  2 green onions, chopped
  2 cloves garlic, chopped
 1/4 teaspoon black pepper
 1/2 teaspoon salt
 1/4 cup Worcestershire sauce
  4 ounces beer
  4 ounces Coca-Cola
  1 2- to 3-pound beef skirt steak

1. Combine all ingredients in a pan large enough to hold steak; marinate at least 4 hours.
2. Cook over hardwood charcoal fire to desired taste (rare, medium, well, etc.).

SERVES 4

SERVING SUGGESTIONS: Try with roasted corn on the cob, mushrooms, or baked potatoes. Very good when rolled in flour tortillas with El Grande Guacamole Salad (page 17).

TEXAS FAJITAS II

A true Tex-Mex specialty.

 1 2-pound beef skirt steak
Salt and black pepper to taste
 2 cloves garlic, finely chopped

1. Remove excess fat from steak and skin membranes. If skirts are thick, split them.
2. Add salt and pepper; rub on garlic.
3. Place seasoned steak in a bowl, cover with foil, and refrigerate at least 12 hours.
4. Place seasoned steak on hot barbecue; cook approximately 4 minutes on one side, turn over and cook approximately 3 minutes on the other side.

SERVES 4

SERVING SUGGESTION: Serve with Frijoles à la Charra (page 127) and Pico de Gallo (page 25).

TACOS AL CARBON

This favorite Tex-Mex dish captures everyone's heart.

 1 recipe Texas Fajitas I or II (page 69)
 1/2 cup vegetable oil
12 flour tortillas
 1/4 cup Pico de Gallo (page 25)

1. Cut barbecued steak into strips.
2. In a cast-iron skillet heat oil and fry tortillas individually.
3. Put strips of meat and a teaspoon of Pico de Gallo on tortilla and roll up. Serve.

SERVES 4

SERVING SUGGESTION: Best with rice and Frijoles à la Charra (page 127).

CHEESE ENCHILADAS

When in the spirit for good Tex-Mex food, this dish is a must. You might even want to trade in your ten-gallon hat for a sombrero.

  1 cup vegetable oil
  2 cups Texas Lightning Chili Gravy (page 24)
 12 corn tortillas
  1 pound cheddar cheese, grated
  1 medium white onion, chopped

1. Heat vegetable oil in a cast-iron skillet.
2. Heat chili gravy in another cast-iron skillet. Preheat oven to 350°.
3. Dip corn tortillas one at a time in hot vegetable oil.
4. Place tortilla in chili gravy for approximately ½ minute; remove tortilla from gravy and lay flat on tray or platter.
5. Put some cheese and onion on one side, slightly off center of tortilla, then roll up tortilla. Repeat process for all tortillas.
6. Place tortillas on baking sheet and pour gravy over them. Top with remaining cheese and onion.
7. Bake enchiladas for 10 minutes or until cheese is melted and enchiladas are hot. Serve immediately.

SERVES 4

SERVING SUGGESTION: Best accompanied by Refried Beans (page 126) and Spanish Rice (page 125).

CHALUPA

This is an easy, traditional Tex-Mex dish.

1 cup vegetable oil
12 corn tortillas
1 cup Refried Beans (page 126)
1 small head lettuce, shredded
1 ripe tomato, diced
1 cup grated cheddar cheese

1. Heat oil in a skillet.
2. Fry corn tortillas separately in hot oil until crisp; drain.
3. On each crisp tortilla, put 1 tablespoon refried beans.
4. Top with lettuce, tomato, and grated cheese. Serve.

SERVES 4

RIO NACHOS

No, this is not the name of a John Wayne movie. But there's a lot of action in the flavor.

1 bag Fritos tortilla chips
1 cup Refried Beans (page 126)
1 green onion, chopped
1 ripe tomato, diced
1 cup grated cheddar cheese
1 8-ounce can sliced jalapeño peppers

1. Preheat oven to 425°.
2. Spread 1 tablespoon refried beans on each chip with ½ teaspoon green onion, ½ teaspoon tomato, ½ teaspoon cheddar cheese.
3. Top with sliced jalapeño pepper.
4. Bake for approximately 8 to 10 minutes, or until cheese is melted.

HUEVOS RANCHEROS

A whole new way to look at eggs—Tex-Mex style.

RANCHERO SAUCE

- 3 *fresh tomatoes*
- 1 *tablespoon vegetable oil*
- 2 *medium onions, diced*
- 2 *fresh jalapeño peppers, seeded and chopped*
- 2 *cloves garlic*
- 2 *cups water*

Salt to taste

- 3 *tablespoons margarine*
- 8 *eggs*

1. Grate tomatoes on a cheese grater. (Throw away skin and stems.) Set aside.
2. In a skillet heat oil and sauté onions, peppers, and garlic until onions are clear.
3. Add fresh tomatoes, water, and salt. Cook approximately 10 minutes.
4. In another skillet melt butter, a little at a time, and fry eggs individually.
5. Cover with sauce and serve.

SERVES 4

SERVING SUGGESTION: Goes best with Refried Beans (page 126).

SUNDAY MORNING OMELET

Actually, this is an every morning omelet. But what better morning of the week is there than Sunday? And that omelet will get you off to a rip-snortin' start.

4 to 6 servings of Quik grits
1/4 cup margarine
4 green onions, chopped
1 tablespoon salt
1 teaspoon black pepper
1/2 teaspoon garlic salt
1/2 pound smoked ham, finely diced
6 eggs, beaten
1/2 cup grated cheddar cheese

1. Keep prepared Quik grits warm in a large pot over low heat.
2. Stir in remaining ingredients and let cook until eggs are done and cheese is melted. Serve.

SERVES 4 TO 6

SERVING SUGGESTION: *Serve with Trailblazer Biscuits (page 132) and jelly.*

TEXAS OMELET

An omelet big enough and flavor-packed enough to be called Texas. Take a bit, and you can almost see the Alamo, Gilley's, and everything else that makes Texas great.

1/4 cup margarine
3 green onions, chopped
1/2 pound ham, diced
2 tablespoons jalapeño pepper, seeded and diced
1/2 teaspoon salt
1/4 teaspoon black pepper
1/8 teaspoon garlic salt
6 eggs, lightly beaten
1/2 cup grated cheddar cheese

1. In a 10-inch skillet melt margarine over medium heat.
2. Add onions, ham, peppers, and seasonings, while stirring; cook until onions are soft.
3. Add eggs and cook until about half done, stirring occasionally.
4. Add cheese and cook until eggs are firm and cheese is melted. (Stir occasionally to prevent sticking.)

SERVES 4

SERVING SUGGESTION: Serve with Gilley's Chili con Carne (page 52), Spanish Rice (page 125), or Refried Beans (page 126).

STAMPEDE EGGS AND CHILI

This breakfast, or anytime dish, just might cause a stampede in your kitchen for more. Boots must be worn in the stampede; hats are optional.

8 Cheese Enchiladas (page 71)
4 cups Gilley's Chili con Carne (page 52) or store-bought or homemade
6 eggs
1/2 teaspoon salt
1/4 teaspoon black pepper
4 green onions, chopped
4 teaspoons margarine
1 cup grated cheddar cheese

1. Preheat oven to 350°.
2. Place enchiladas in shallow pan and warm them in hot oven.
3. Place chili in a small saucepan, and warm over low heat.
4. Beat eggs lightly in a small bowl with salt, pepper, and green onions.
5. In a 10-inch skillet melt margarine over medium heat and scramble eggs.
6. Divide scrambled eggs evenly on four oven-safe 10-inch platters and place two hot enchiladas on each platter.
7. Cover each serving with chili and sprinkle with grated cheese.
8. Place platters in the oven and bake for 5 minutes at 350°.

SERVES 4

RANCHER'S BREAKFAST

When you taste this Texas rancher's delight, you'll yearn for the wide open spaces and Texas cookin'.

    2 eggs
    2 tablespoons cornmeal
    1 teaspoon salt
  1/8 teaspoon black pepper
1 1/2 pounds calves' brains, sliced
    4 tablespoons margarine

1. Mix eggs, cornmeal, salt, and pepper in a bowl.
2. Add brains and mix well.
3. In a heavy skillet melt margarine and cook brains for 10 minutes over medium heat. Stir constantly to prevent sticking.

SERVES 2

SERVING SUGGESTIONS: Serve with Hachamore Hominy (page 127), Gilley's Chili con Carne (page 52), or sausages and sourdough biscuits, or Not-So-Quiet Hush Puppies (page 133).

AUSTIN OMELETTE

Try this country fresh recipe to start off your day . . . or even to end it after a night at the honky-tonks.

  3 tablespoons margarine
  8 ounces chopped chicken livers
  6 eggs
 $1/4$ cup buttermilk
 $1/2$ teaspoon salt
 $1/8$ teaspoon black pepper

1. In skillet heat margarine and brown chicken livers lightly.
2. Combine eggs, buttermilk, salt, and pepper in bowl, and beat well.
3. Pour egg mixture over liver, and cook at low heat while stirring until eggs are set.

SERVES 2 TO 4

4

FOR HUNTERS ONLY: DELECTABLE GAME

A Few Words on Wild Game Cooking from Pat Wright

Texas is fortunate in having one of the finest parks and wildlife departments in North America. As a result, the state and its coastal waters abound with fish and wild game. If you were to go through Gilley's on any Saturday night and ask all the old hands, "What are the three most important pleasures in life?" the most popular answer would probably be, "Fishin', huntin', and lovin'." So a Texas cookbook wouldn't be complete without some wild game recipes.

There are many gourmet supermarkets and fine meat markets that offer domestically-raised wild game and fowl that make excellent table fare for those who prefer to do their hunting with a shopping cart. If you are blessed with a family member or a friend who is a hunter, and will share his bag limit with you (in which case, you can consider him a damn good friend), you're half way there. But the second half is the most important—the care taken in cleaning, storing, and preparing wild meat that is taken in the field.

Deer should be bled, skinned, drawn, cleaned with cool water, and cooled immediately after the kill. Inspect and remove all hair that might be clinging to the meat. When you see a deer hanging on the fender of a truck or car while the hunter drives four or five hours in 60° or above temperature to the house, just so everyone will know he "got one," you can bet that meat ain't going to taste worth a damn when it hits somebody's mouth.

If possible, the carcass should hang in cold storage at 36–40°: young animals for one week, older animals for two or three weeks. If this is not possible, quarter the deer and store it in an ice chest with frozen plastic bottles of water while transporting. When processing, butcher the same as beef, removing all fat. Wash with cold water and store all meat that is to be frozen in zip-lock freezer bags. Refrigerated meat that is to be cooked may not be stored any longer than beef would be stored.

Some people find the "wild taste" in venison too strong for their taste. Before cooking, soak meat overnight in salted water (two tablespoons per quart) to mellow the meat.

Small game needs the same care in cleaning. There are scent glands under forelegs and on the lower back near the spine that must be removed. Soak overnight in salt water before cooking or freezing.

Game birds may be plucked or skinned. Always draw birds as soon as possible after the kill, and keep cool in transporting. Soak overnight in salt water before freezing.

Of course, the best way to learn processing and caring for wild game is to buddy-up to an experienced hunter and pick his brain. Good sportsmen are always willing to share their hard-earned wisdom.

BRAIDED BIRD AND BAYOU

This is a delicacy just for seafood lovers. And if you're not a seafood lover, try this and you'll become one.

$^1/_4$ cup margarine

  4 quail breasts, cut in $^1/_2$-inch strips

16 shelled jumbo shrimp

  1 8-ounce can sliced mushrooms, drained

$^1/_4$ cup chopped yellow onion

$^1/_2$ teaspoon salt

$^1/_4$ teaspoon black pepper

$^1/_8$ teaspoon garlic salt

$^1/_2$ teaspoon parsley flakes

Juice of 1 lemon

$^1/_2$ cup sangria

1. Melt margarine in a large skillet.
2. Combine all ingredients, except wine, in skillet and cook over medium heat, until breasts and shrimp are tender.
3. Add wine, stir, and simmer over low heat for 20 minutes.

SERVES 4

SERVING SUGGESTION: *Serve over Ranch Rice (page 123) with green garden vegetable.*

CAMP BOSS QUAIL

Once you serve this dish, there will be no doubt as to who's the boss in your camp or kitchen.

2 cups flour
1 tablespoon salt
1/2 teaspoon black pepper
1/4 cup margarine
8 whole quails
1 cup cooking sherry
2 cans chicken noodle soup
2 green onions, chopped

1. Combine flour, salt, and pepper in a bowl.
2. Roll quail in flour mix and shake off excess flour.
3. In a large skillet melt margarine and brown all sides of quail lightly over medium heat.
4. Add sherry, soup, and onions, cover and simmer over low heat for 30 minutes, or until quails are tender.

SERVES 4 TO 6

SERVING SUGGESTION: Serve with Ranch Rice (page 123) and green garden vegetables.

PLUM GOOD QUAIL

The name of this dish describes the treat that's in store for you.

½ cup margarine
1 cup cooking sherry
Juice of 1 lemon
1 teaspoon salt
½ teaspoon black pepper
2 fresh pears, quartered and core removed
8 medium-size plums
8 fresh Bing cherries
8 whole quails

1. Preheat oven to 450°.
2. In a saucepan combine margarine, sherry, lemon, salt, and pepper. Heat to simmer and keep warm.
3. Dip fruit in sauce.
4. Place a pear slice, a plum, and a cherry in cavity of each bird.
5. Place quails in roasting pan and baste well with sauce.
6. Bake about 30 minutes until tender and crisp, basting and turning about every 5 minutes. (May also be cooked over hardwood charcoal fire.)

SERVES 4 TO 6

ADOBE DOVE KABOB

This dish may be a tongue twister to say, but after tasting it, you might not want to say anything else. Most cowboys take to this like a bow to a fiddle.

 1 *16-ounce bottle Italian dressing*
 1 *clove garlic, diced*
 4 *ounces Worcestershire sauce*
16 *dove breasts*
 8 *large mushrooms*
 4 *10-inch wood skewers*
 2 *large bell peppers, quartered*
 2 *small onions, quartered*
 8 *cherry tomatoes*
 4 *large stuffed green olives*

1. Mix Italian dressing, garlic and Worcestershire sauce in a 2-inch-deep pan. Marinate dove and mushrooms for at least 4 hours (or overnight).
2. Skewer on wood sticks in this order: dove breast, mushroom, bell pepper, breast, onion, tomato, breast, mushroom, bell pepper, breast, onion, tomato, and olive.
3. Either charcoal broil over an open fire or broil in oven, basting with marinade every 3 to 4 minutes while cooking and turning. Cook to taste (well, medium, rare, etc.).

SERVES 4

SERVING SUGGESTION: Best served on a bed of Ranch Rice (page 123).

DAMN GOOD DOVE BREAST

What is there left to say after damn good? Dove breast, naturally. This treat just might be the change of pace that a "steak and potatoes" guy needs. Of course, for the little buckaroos, this dish is called "darn good dove breast."

1/2 cup vegetable oil
1 cup flour
1/4 teaspoon black pepper
1/2 teaspoon salt
1/4 teaspoon garlic salt
1 tablespoon baking powder
16 dove breasts
1/2 onion, chopped
1 cup milk

1. Heat vegetable oil to 375° (medium heat) in a large skillet.
2. Combine dry ingredients in a bowl.
3. Roll dove breasts until completely covered with flour mix.
4. Place in skillet and brown lightly. Remove dove and set aside.
5. Add onions and 4 tablespoons flour mix to hot grease. Brown lightly.
6. Add milk and stir constantly until creamy smooth. (If too thick, add water.)
7. Return breast to skillet. Cover and simmer at low heat for approximately 30 minutes, or until breasts are tender.

SERVES 4

SERVING SUGGESTION: Serve over bed of Ranch Rice (page 123).

DOUGH WRANGLER DOVE

This seasoned dove is ideal for any time of year.

  1 *cup flour*
  1 *teaspoon salt*
$^1/_2$ *teaspoon black pepper*
  8 *doves or dove breasts*
$^1/_4$ *cup margarine*
  4 *cups warm Ranch Rice (page 123) or any cooked rice*
  2 *cans cream of chicken mushroom soup, slightly diluted*

1. Combine flour, salt, and pepper in a bowl.
2. Roll dove in flour mix and shake off excess mix.
3. Heat magarine in a skillet over medium heat and brown dove on all sides.
4. Remove dove and place in a large casserole dish, then cover with Ranch Rice. Preheat oven to 350°.
5. Heat soup in a skillet until warm and smooth; pour over dove and rice.
6. Bake, uncovered, for 30 minutes.

SERVES 4

SERVING SUGGESTION: Serve with Feed Bag Fritters (page 113) and green garden vegetable.

GOLD NUGGET DOVE

Strike your claim on this one.

¹/₂ cup bread crumbs
¹/₄ cup Parmesan cheese
1 teaspoon salt
¹/₄ teaspoon black pepper
1 teaspoon crushed sweet basil
1 teaspoon parsley flakes
¹/₈ teaspoon garlic salt
8 dove breasts
¹/₂ cup melted margarine

1. Preheat oven to 400°.
2. Combine bread crumbs, cheese, and seasonings in a bowl.
3. Dip each breast in melted margarine, then roll in crumbs.
4. Place on foil-lined baking sheet and bake for approximately 15 minutes, or until golden brown.

SERVES 4

SERVING SUGGESTION: Best accompanied by Trailblazer Biscuits (page 132), gravy, and green garden vegetables.

HONDO DOVE

This recipe can be used with all small game birds and ducks. It's a nice dish to prepare for those special occasions.

1 lemon, halved
8 whole doves
Salt and black pepper to taste
2 small yellow onions, quartered
2 small potatoes, peeled and quartered
1/4 cup melted margarine
8 thick-sliced strips smoked slab bacon

1. Preheat oven to 425°.
2. Rub lemon halves over dove, and squeeze a little into each cavity.
3. Salt and pepper dove inside and outside.
4. Dip a piece of onion and a piece of potato into melted margarine and stuff into cavity of each bird.
5. Wrap each dove with 1 bacon strip and secure with toothpick. Place each dove on a piece of aluminum foil big enough to wrap dove.
6. Pour about 2 tablespoons melted margarine over each dove and close foil, covering each bird completely.
7. Place wrapped doves on cooking sheet and place in oven for 30 to 45 minutes, or until doves are tender.

SERVES 4

SERVING SUGGESTION: Serve with Hachamore Hominy (page 127) and a green garden vegetable.

DAY LAKE DUCK

A really simple—but sensational—duck dish.

2 mallard breasts, filleted and cut into 4 pieces each
¹/₄ cup melted margarine
Garlic salt
Black pepper
1 can (8) refrigerated buttermilk biscuits
8 1¹/₂" × 1¹/₂" slices Swiss cheese
4 cups warm Six-Shooter Cream Sauce (page 27) or any white sauce

1. Preheat oven to 450°.
2. Dip duck fillets in melted margarine.
3. Season all over with garlic salt and pepper to taste.
4. Place in a shallow pan and bake for 15 minutes.
5. Press out biscuits until they're 4 or 5 inches across and place 1 piece of cheese on each biscuit.
6. Dip fillets in margarine again and place on biscuit. Wrap biscuit and cheese around fillet, covering as well as possible.
7. Place on a foil-lined baking sheet with biscuit seam down and bake for 8 to 10 minutes, or until biscuits are golden brown.
8. Pour cream sauce over each portion before serving.

SERVES 4

SERVING SUGGESTION: Serve with Ranch Rice (page 123) or whipped potatoes and a garden vegetable.

FANDANGO DUCK

This duck delicacy will get you in the mood for a night of dancing, whether it's the fandango or two-step.

$^1/_2$ cup margarine
4 tablespoons light Karo syrup
1 teaspoon salt
$^1/_2$ teaspoon black pepper
$^1/_2$ teaspoon cinnamon
2 large or 4 small ducks
3 to 4 large oranges, peeled and sectioned
1 6-ounce can unsweetened orange juice
1 16-ounce can cooked sweet potatoes

1. Melt margarine, syrup, and seasonings in a saucepan and keep warm. Preheat oven to 325°.
2. Salt and pepper ducks lightly on the inside and outside.
3. Stuff orange sections into cavity of each bird and place in a roasting pan.
4. Pour sauce and orange juice over birds.
5. Cover and bake for 1 hour.
6. Add sweet potatoes, cover, and bake for 30 more minutes.
7. Uncover and cook until duck browns on top side and potatoes are glazed.

SERVES 4

SERVING SUGGESTION: Serve with Ranch Rice (page 123) and a spinach salad.

LITTLE DARLING DUCK

Fix your favorite cowgirl this delicious duck dish. If she's not your little darling now, she will be with just one taste.

  3 cups hot water
  1 teaspoon salt
  $1/2$ teaspoon black pepper
  1 large duck, cut into serving pieces
  $1/2$ cup peeled sliced carrots
  $1/4$ cup sliced celery
  $1/4$ cup diced green peppers
  3 cups milk
  1 can chicken noodle soup
  1 can cream of mushroom soup

1. Combine first 7 ingredients in a large pot and bring to a slow boil.
2. Reduce heat, cover, and simmer over low heat until carrots are fairly tender.
3. Stir in milk and soups and bring back to a simmer for 10 to 15 minutes.

SERVES 4

SERVING SUGGESTION: Try with Corral Corn Bread (page 130) or Feed Bag Fritters (page 113).

WOODWAY DUCK

Here's yet another way to fix that fresh duck.

1 *plump young mallard, cut in serving pieces*
Salt and black pepper to taste
1 *cup crushed pineapple in heavy syrup*
$^1/_4$ *cup prepared mustard*
$^1/_2$ *cup diced chutney*
$^1/_2$ *cup chopped pecans*
$^1/_2$ *cup frozen blackberries, thawed*

1. Preheat oven to 350°.
2. Salt and pepper duck all over and place in a casserole dish.
3. Combine remaining ingredients in a bowl, mix well, and pour over duck.
4. Bake, uncovered, for 1$^1/_4$ hours.

SERVES 4

GALVESTON STUFFED GOOSE

You'll be tempted to stuff yourself with this dandy goose dish.

  1 8- to 10-pound goose
Juice of 1 lemon
Salt and black pepper to taste
1/4 cup margarine
  1 large head cabbage, shredded
  1 large onion, sliced
  1 large apple, cored and sliced
  1 cup red wine
  2 tablespoons Italian dressing
  1 tablespoon sugar
1/2 teaspoon paprika
  8 strips smoked slab bacon

1. Dry goose and rub with lemon juice inside and out. Season with salt and black pepper.
2. In a large pot melt margarine and sauté all remaining ingredients except bacon until cabbage is wilted.
3. Preheat oven to 350°.
4. Drain off excess juice and stuff mixture into goose cavity. Close cavity with string and skewers.
5. Place goose in a roasting pan with breast side up and cover with bacon strips.
6. Pour excess juice over goose and bake for 20 minutes per pound, or until goose is tender.

SERVES 4 TO 6

SERVING SUGGESTION: Serve with Corral Corn Bread (page 130) and a green garden vegetable.

GLADEWATER GOOSE

For goose lovers on the go, this dish is a breeze to prepare.

1 *large goose breast, filleted and cubed into 1-inch pieces*
1 *can cream of mushroom soup*
1 *cup red wine*
1 *cup sliced fresh mushrooms*
1 *package onion soup mix*
2 *tablespoons parsley flakes*

Combine all ingredients in a pot and simmer over low heat until goose and mushrooms are very tender.

SERVES 4

SERVING SUGGESTION: Best with Ranch Rice (page 123) and Polk County Collards (page 111).

TALL-WILLOW TEAL

The kind of recipe you'd write home to mother about.

  8 *teal or wood duck breasts, filleted*
Salt and black pepper to taste
  1 *cup flour*
¼ cup margarine
  1 *16-ounce can stewed tomatoes (preferably Ro-tel)*
½ cup water
  3 *tablespoons dark Karo syrup*
  2 *tablespoons Italian dressing*
  3 *tablespoons Worcestershire sauce*
  1 *teaspoon salt*
  1 *teaspoon chili powder*
  1 *teaspoon dry mustard*
  1 *clove garlic, finely diced*
½ teaspoon celery salt

1. Season breasts with salt and pepper, then roll fillets in flour.
2. In a large heavy skillet or Dutch oven melt margarine and brown fillets over medium heat. Remove and set aside.
3. Combine remaining ingredients in the skillet. Stir and bring to a boil.
4. Return breasts to skillet, reduce heat to simmer, cover, and cook 40 to 45 minutes until duck is tender.

SERVES 4

SERVING SUGGESTION: Serve with Ranch Rice and Corral Corn Bread (pages 123 and 130).

PALMETTO PENTAIL

Good eatin' is in the palm of your hand with palmetto pentail.

1/4 cup margarine
8 pentail breasts, filleted and cut into 1/2-inch strips seasoned with salt and black pepper to taste
Juice of 1/2 lemon
3 tablespoons chopped fresh parsley
2 green onions, chopped
1/2 teaspoon sage

1. In a large skillet melt margarine and brown fillets lightly over medium heat.
2. Add remaining ingredients, stirring often to prevent sticking. Cook until fillets are tender.

SERVES 4

SERVING SUGGESTION: Serve on bed of Ranch Rice (page 123) with a green garden vegetable.

BIG THICKET BUCK

Savory good eating.

  3 *pounds venison leg, shoulder, or rump, cut into 1¹/₂-inch*
      cubes
  1 *cup flour*
¹/₄ *cup margarine*
  6 *green onions, chopped*
  1 *bell pepper, diced*
  1 *tablespoon paprika*
  1 *teaspoon salt*
¹/₂ *teaspoon black pepper*
  2 *cups hot water*
  8 *ounces sour cream*
  1 *can cream of mushroom soup*
  2 *cups diced potatoes*

1. Roll venison in flour.
2. In a large pot or Dutch oven melt margarine and sauté venison, onions, bell pepper, seasonings, and flour over medium heat until lightly brown.
3. Stir in hot water, sour cream, and soup. Increase heat and bring to a boil.
4. Reduce heat and simmer until venison is fairly tender.
5. Add potatoes and simmer until potatoes are tender. Serve.

SERVES 4 TO 6

BRUSH COUNTRY FRIED BACKSTRAP

Here's a dream dish for all you deer lovers. But this recipe can be used for frying filleted duck breast, young squirrel, young rabbit, dove and quail breast, goose breast, fish, frog legs, seafood, or any other tender cut of wild game, too.

  2 cups flour
  1/2 teaspoon black pepper
  1 teaspoon baking powder
  1/4 teaspoon garlic salt
  1 teaspoon parsley flakes
  2 cups buttermilk
  4 cups water
  4 tablespoons salt
  2 pounds venison tenderloin fillets, sliced 1/2 inch thick
  4 cups vegetable oil

1. Combine flour, pepper, baking powder, garlic salt, and parsley flakes in a large bowl and mix thoroughly.
2. In a separate large bowl, combine buttermilk, water, and salt, and mix well.
3. Roll fillets in flour mix, then dip fillets into batter and let excess batter drain off.
4. Return fillets to flour mix and roll; shake off excess flour.
5. In a large skillet or Dutch oven heat oil until very hot and drop fillets individually into skillet. Cook over medium heat until golden brown.

SERVES 4 TO 6

SERVING SUGGESTION: Best with Trailblazer Biscuits (page 132), Six-Shooter Cream Sauce (page 27), and Ranch Rice (page 123) or mashed potatoes.

CHOPPED BUCK STEAKS

You're on the right track for some good barbecued wild game when you fix these steaks. It's almost as much fun fixing this dish as it is eating it.

2 pounds coarsely ground or finely chopped venison
1/4 cup Worcestershire sauce
1 yellow onion, diced
1 teaspoon salt
1/2 teaspoon black pepper
1/8 teaspoon garlic salt
1/2 cup beer
4 tablespoons lard
1/4 cup melted margarine
8 strips thick-sliced smoked bacon

1. Combine all ingredients except bacon in a bowl and blend thoroughly.
2. Form into 8 patties and wrap with bacon and secure with toothpicks.
3. Cook over hardwood charcoal fire or in a skillet over low heat for 12 to 15 minutes. Baste with margarine each time patties are turned.

SERVES 6 TO 8

SERVING SUGGESTION: *Serve with any biscuits, gravy, and green garden vegetables.*

DALLIED BACKSTRAP

Wrap this around your fork. Um-m-m-m-m!

   6 to 8 venison tenderloin fillets, 1¹/₂ inch thick
   6 to 8 strips salt pork, ¹/₄ inch thick
   1 recipe Sweet Iron Steak Baste (page 29)

1. Wrap fillets with salt pork strips and secure with toothpicks.
2. Dip fillets in baste and cook over hardwood charcoal fire for 4 to 5 minutes on each side, or to taste (medium, well, etc.), basting frequently.

SERVES 4

SERVING SUGGESTION: Serve with Ranch Rice (page 123), baked potatoes or roasted ears of corn, and a green garden vegetable.

SADDLEBREAD VENISON

You'll be riding tall in the saddle after a meal of this tasty, tender venison.

1 2-pound venison steak, 1 inch thick
1/2 cup flour
1/4 cup margarine
1 yellow onion, sliced
1 bell pepper, sliced
1 cup diced celery
1 8-ounce can peeled tomatoes
1 can beef bouillon soup
1 teaspoon salt
1/2 teaspoon black pepper
1/2 teaspoon crushed sweet basil

1. Roll steak in flour.
2. In a large heavy skillet melt margarine and brown steak lightly over medium heat.
3. Remove steak, stir in remaining ingredients, and place steaks on top.
4. Cover and simmer for approximately 1½ hours, until meat is tender.

SERVES 4

SERVING SUGGESTION: Terrific with Ranch Rice (page 123), Granny's Squash and Squash (page 119), and Corral Corn Bread (page 130).

CALICO COTTONTAIL

Just wait till you sit down to this flavorful rabbit.

2 *eggs, beaten*
1 *teaspoon salt*
1/2 *teaspoon black pepper*
2 *cottontails or young swamp rabbits, cut into serving pieces*
  with rib cage removed
2 *cups bread crumbs*
1/4 *cup margarine*
1 *can cream of chicken soup*
6 *ounces water*
1 *yellow onion, sliced*

1. Combine eggs, salt, and pepper in a bowl.
2. Dip pieces of rabbit in bowl, let excess batter drain off, then roll rabbit in bread crumbs.
3. In a large skillet melt margarine, brown rabbit pieces lightly on all sides over medium heat. Remove rabbit and place in a roasting pan or a long casserole dish. Preheat oven to 350°.
4. Combine soup, water, and onion in the skillet; heat and stir until well-blended and pour over rabbit.
5. Bake approximately 50 to 60 minutes, or until rabbit is tender.

SERVES 4 TO 6

SERVING SUGGESTION: Serve with Ranch Rice (page 123) and green garden vegetables.

ROUGH RIDER RABBIT

This dish will almost turn any cowboy into a hunter, just so he can bag a rabbit and turn this meal into a feast.

1/4 cup margarine
1 medium-size rabbit, cut into 8 pieces
1/2 yellow onion, chopped
1 teaspoon salt
1/4 teaspoon black pepper
3 cups apple cider
1 apple, sliced
1/2 cup raisins
4 tablespoons dark Karo syrup
1 cup uncooked long-grain rice

1. In a large skillet melt margarine and sauté rabbit, onion, and seasonings over medium heat 5 to 8 minutes until onions are soft.
2. Add cider, increase heat, and bring to a slow boil.
3. Reduce heat to low, cover, and simmer until rabbit is fairly tender. Increase heat and return to a boil.
4. Add apples, raisins, syrup, and rice, and stir.
5. Reduce heat and simmer approximately 20 minutes, or until liquid is absorbed and rice is tender.

SERVES 4 TO 6

HOG-TIED SQUIRREL

If you're going to cook squirrel, there's no better way than this.
But this recipe also is great for rabbit, duck, quail, or pheasant.

4 *whole young squirrels*
8 *cups water*
3 *teaspoons salt*
1 *teaspoon black pepper*
4 *cups Doughbelly Dressing (page 31)*
2 *cans cream of chicken mushroom soup*

1. Place squirrels, water, salt, and pepper in a pot and bring to a boil.
2. Reduce heat and simmer until squirrels are tender. Remove squirrels and let stand until cool enough to handle. Preheat oven to 350°.
3. Stuff chest cavity of each squirrel with 1 cup dressing. Secure front legs to back legs with wet cotton string encircling dressing to help hold it in place.
4. Place stuffed squirrels in a large casserole dish or roasting pan.
5. Combine 8 ounces of stock from boiling pot with soup and blend well.
6. Pour over squirrels and bake for 30 minutes, or until bubbling hot.

SERVES 4 TO 6

5

HIGH NOON OR ANYTIME SIDE DISHES

COWPOKE CABBAGE

Bet you never knew cabbage could taste so good.

    1 head cabbage, shredded
    1 cup water
    1 teaspoon salt
  $^1/_4$ teaspoon black pepper
    1 cup grated cheddar cheese
  1$^1/_2$ cup any white sauce or Six-Shooter Cream Sauce (page 27)
    1 cup cracker crumbs

1. In a 2-quart casserole cook cabbage in water until soft. Drain off water. Preheat oven to 350°.
2. Stir in salt and pepper.
3. Pour cheese and white sauce over cabbage.
4. Top with cracker crumbs and bake for 20 minutes.

SERVES 4 TO 6

POLK COUNTY COLLARDS

If you're going to fix collards, turnips, or mustard greens this is the way. This country-flavored collards recipe is a great dish to fix when you get that down-home feeling.

¹/₄ cup margarine
6 ounces smoked slab bacon with rind or salt pork, thick sliced
¹/₂ yellow onion, diced
1 to 2 tablespoons salt
1 teaspoon black pepper
¹/₈ teaspoon celery salt
3 cups hot water
Approximately 2 pounds fresh collard greens, washed and drained

1. In a skillet melt margarine and sauté bacon, onions, and seasonings over medium heat for 8 minutes.
2. Add water, increase heat to high, and bring to a boil.
3. Stir in collards until wilted.
4. Reduce heat to low and simmer until the greens are tender.

SERVES 4 TO 6

CHEROKEE CORN

This dish is a corn lover's delight—made with cheddar cheese and jalapeños to give it that unforgettable flavor.

- ½ cup margarine
- 2 16-ounce cans cream-style corn
- 1 teaspoon garlic salt
- 2 eggs
- ¾ cup yellow cornmeal
- ½ cup diced canned jalapeños
- 2 cups grated cheddar cheese

1. Preheat oven to 350°.
2. Mix all ingredients in a 2-quart casserole, saving a little cheese for topping.
3. Top with remaining cheese and bake for 1 hour.

SERVES 6 TO 8

FEED BAG FRITTERS

Got the munchies? These corn fritters are for you.

$1/2$ cup yellow cornmeal
1 cup flour
2 teaspoons baking powder
$1/2$ teaspoon salt
$1/4$ teaspoon black pepper
$1/4$ cup sugar
1 egg, beaten
$1/3$ cup milk
2 teaspoons melted shortening
1 16-ounce can whole-kernel corn, drained
$1/2$ cup finely diced yellow onion
4 cups vegetable oil

1. Combine first 6 ingredients in a large bowl.
2. Stir in remaining ingredients and blend until smooth.
3. In a skillet heat oil.
4. Drop mixture by spoonfuls in hot oil over medium heat until fritters float and become golden brown.

SERVES 4 TO 6

DRY CREEK FRIED GREEN TOMATOES

Although it's called "Dry Creek," this dish will make your mouth water. This delight is easy to rustle up, and it just might entice a cowboy to trade in his six-gallon hat for a chef's hat. But not likely.

1 egg
1 cup buttermilk
2/3 cup flour
1 teaspoon salt
1/4 teaspoon black pepper
1/4 teaspoon baking powder
1/8 teaspoon garlic salt
4 large green tomatoes, quartered
3 cups vegetable oil

1. In a bowl beat egg lightly with fork, and stir in buttermilk, flour, and seasonings.
2. Dip tomato quarters into batter and let excess drain off.
3. In a skillet heat oil; place tomatoes in hot oil one piece at a time, frying to golden brown at 375° (medium heat).

SERVES 4 TO 6

SERVING SUGGESTION: *Cover with Six-Shooter Cream Sauce (page 27) for an added taste treat.*

OXBOW FRIED OKRA

If you're aimin' for some okay okra, try it fried. What a dish.

$^1/_2$ cup flour
$^1/_2$ cup yellow cornmeal
$^1/_2$ teaspoon black pepper
$^1/_2$ teaspoon garlic salt
 2 eggs
 1 cup buttermilk
 2 tablespoons salt
 1 pound fresh okra, sliced
 4 cups vegetable oil

1. Combine flour, cornmeal, pepper, and garlic salt in medium-size paper bag.
2. Combine eggs, buttermilk, and salt in a bowl and beat well.
3. Place about half of the okra in the batter; scoop out and let excess batter drain off.
4. Place in flour bag and shake well.
5. Heat oil in a skillet and drop okra in hot oil carefully. Cook until golden brown.

SERVES 4

ACE-IN-THE-HOLE OKRA

This is every cook's ace in the hole. You'll always have the winning hand when you serve this dish.

$1/4$ cup margarine
 4 green onions, chopped
 1 bell pepper, diced
 1 pound fresh okra, cut up, or 1 package frozen okra
 1 teaspoon salt
$1/2$ teaspoon black pepper
$1/8$ teaspoon celery salt
$1/8$ teaspoon red (cayenne) pepper
 1 tablespoon maple syrup
 1 16-ounce can stewed tomatoes
 1 8-ounce can tomato sauce

1. In a large pot or Dutch oven melt margarine and sauté onions, bell pepper, okra, and seasonings over medium heat for about 5 to 8 minutes.
2. Add syrup, tomatoes, and tomato sauce. Bring to a boil.
3. Reduce heat, cover, and simmer for 8 minutes.

SERVES 6 TO 8

SERVING SUGGESTION: Tasty served with steamed rice.

SOURDOUGH ONION RINGS

Is this any way to treat an onion? You bet it is! Try it.

2 cups flour
$1/4$ teaspoon black pepper
$1/8$ teaspoon garlic salt
3 tablespoons salt
1 cup buttermilk
1 cup water
2 large yellow onions, sliced and rings separated
3 cups vegetable oil

1. In a bowl combine flour, pepper, and garlic salt.
2. In another bowl combine salt, buttermilk, and water.
3. Dip onion rings in batter first then into flour mix, covering completely. Repeat.
4. In a skillet heat oil and drop rings individually into hot oil over medium heat. Fry until golden brown.

SERVES 4 TO 6

BOTTOMLAND YAMS

Yes, ma'am. These yams are for you and your buckaroo.

    4 cups sliced cooked sweet potatoes
  1/2 cup dark Karo syrup
  1/2 cup melted margarine
    1 teaspoon salt
  1/8 teaspoon black pepper
    1 cup chopped pecans
    2 tablespoons cinnamon

1. Preheat oven to 350°.
2. Combine all ingredients, except cinnamon, in a 2-quart casserole. Top with cinnamon.
3. Bake, uncovered, for 20 minutes.

SERVES 4 TO 6

GRANNY'S SQUASH AND SQUASH

After tasting this super squash, it'll surefire become your favorite squash dish.

4 tablespoons margarine
4 acorn squash, cubed
2 yellow squash, sliced into 1/4-inch pieces
1/2 bell pepper, diced
1/8 teaspoon black pepper
1/8 teaspoon celery salt
1 teaspoon salt
1 8-ounce can tomato sauce
1/4 cup Parmesan cheese

1. In a skillet melt margarine and sauté squash for 5 minutes over medium heat.
2. Add remaining ingredients, cover, and cook over low heat about 15 minutes, until squash is tender.

SERVES 4 TO 6

BAKED TURNIPS

This recipe for turnips will turn up some great eatin'.

 2 pounds small turnips
$1/4$ cup melted margarine
$1/2$ teaspoon salt
$1/4$ teaspoon coarse black pepper
$1/8$ teaspoon garlic powder

1. Wash and trim turnips.
2. In a pot boil turnips in enough water to cover for 20 minutes, or until you can stick them with a fork.
3. Place turnips in a shallow baking pan, baste with margarine, and sprinkle with seasonings.
4. Cover and bake at 400° for 30 minutes.

SERVES 4 TO 6

OLD-FASHIONED SWEET POTATO PIE

This dish is destined to become one of your family's favorites.

  3 *eggs, beaten*
  1 *cup sugar*
  1 *cup mashed, cooked sweet potatoes*
  1 *cup half-and-half or evaporated milk*
$1/4$ *cup butter, melted*
$1/2$ *teaspoon allspice*
$1/2$ *teaspoon cinnamon*
$1/2$ *teaspoon nutmeg*
$1/2$ *teaspoon salt*
  1 *unbaked Standard Pie Shell (page 144) or store-bought*
    9-inch shell

1. Preheat oven to 400°F.
2. Blend all ingredients.
3. Pour into uncooked pie shell and bake for 10 minutes.
4. Reduce heat to 350° and bake until knife inserted in center comes out clean.

HONKY-TONK HAM AND PINEAPPLE DELIGHT

You can ham it up in the food department with this marvelous delight.

   6 slices fresh or canned pineapple
   2 cups ground cooked ham (see Note)
  1/4 cup milk for ham and
   2 tablespoons for yams
   1 tablespoon mustard
   2 cups mashed yams
  1/2 cup melted butter
   6 large marshmallows

1. Preheat oven to 350°.
2. Place pineapple slices in a greased 9"- × -9"- × -2" pan.
3. In a bowl mix ham with 1/4 cup milk and mustard to form 6 patties. Put mixture on top of each pineapple slice.
4. In another bowl mix yams, butter, and 2 tablespoons milk together and place on top of ham mixture.
5. Bake for 30 minutes.
6. Remove from oven and place a marshmallow on top of each mound. Return to oven and bake at 350° for 2 to 3 minutes.

SERVES 6

NOTE: Six slices of ham 1/4 inch thick can be substituted for ground ham. Omit 1/4 cup milk and mustard.

RANCH RICE

Simple and versatile, this rice dish is the perfect accompaniment to almost any meal.

1/4 cup margarine
1/2 cup diced onions
1/4 teaspoon black pepper
1/2 teaspoon salt
1/4 cup Worcestershire sauce
1/8 teaspoon garlic salt
 2 cups hot water
 1 cup uncooked long-grain rice

1. In a 2-quart pot melt margarine and sauté onions with seasonings for 3 to 4 minutes over medium heat.
2. Add hot water and bring to a boil over high heat.
3. Stir in rice and return to a boil.
4. Cover and simmer for 15 to 20 minutes, until water is all absorbed and rice is tender. (No peeping first 15 minutes.)

SERVES 4 TO 6

BUCKBOARD BEANS AND RICE

You'll get hitched up to some fine Texas eatin' when you try this tangy recipe for beans and rice. It takes a while to make, but it's worth it!

4   ounces smoked slab bacon, thick sliced
1/2 yellow onion, diced
2   teaspoons salt
1/2 teaspoon black pepper
1/2 teaspoon red (cayenne) pepper
1/4 cup Worcestershire sauce
1/4 teaspoon celery salt
1   clove garlic, diced
4   cups hot water
2   cups dried pinto beans
4   cups Ranch Rice (page 123) or cooked long-grain rice

1. Cook bacon in a 5-quart pot until grease is well-released.
2. Add onions and seasonings, and sauté for about 8 minutes over low heat.
3. Add hot water and beans, increase heat, and bring to a boil.
4. Reduce heat, cover, and simmer for 3 to 4 hours, or until beans are tender.
5. Serve poured over rice.

SERVES 4 TO 6

SERVING SUGGESTION: Best with Corral or Caliente Corn Bread (pages 130 and 131), or Feed Bag Fritters (page 113).

SPANISH RICE

This dish goes great with almost any Spanish dish.

1 *cup uncooked white rice*
1/2 *medium onion, chopped*
1 *8-ounce can tomato sauce*
1 *clove of garlic, chopped*
3 *cups water*
1 *bouillon cube made into chicken broth according to package directions*
1/2 *medium bell pepper, sliced in half*
1/3 *teaspoon black pepper*

1. Brown rice in pan using a small amount of grease.
2. Drain excess grease.
3. Add onion and brown slightly.
4. Add tomato sauce and garlic. Let fry.
5. Add 3 cups of water and bring to boil.
6. After water boils, add broth, bell pepper, and black pepper.
7. After mixture returns to a boil, turn heat down, and cover (do not stir).
8. Rice is ready when water has evaporated.

REFRIED BEANS

A Mexican dinner just wouldn't be complete without this delectable dish.

2 cups dried pinto beans, cleaned
Salt to taste
2 cups vegetable oil
1 onion, chopped
1 jalapeño pepper, seeded and chopped (optional)
1 clove garlic

1. Boil beans with salt in sufficient water to cover approximately 4 hours, or until beans are tender.
2. Heat oil in a skillet and sauté onion, jalapeño, and garlic.
3. Pour skillet mixture with hot oil in beans.
4. Mash with potato masher. Beans will absorb all the oil when they are mashed smooth.

SERVES 6

FRIJOLES À LA CHARRA

Good enough for a meal in itself.

  2 cups raw pinto beans, cleaned
Salt to taste
¹/₂ pound bacon (ends and pieces are fine), diced
  1 onion, diced
  1 jalapeño pepper, seeded and chopped
¹/₂ bunch cilantro, chopped

1. In a pot cook pinto beans with enough water to cover and salt
   for approximately 4 hours, until done. Set aside.
2. Put bacon pieces in a skillet and fry until half done.
3. Add onion, jalapeño, and cilantro and sauté approximately 4
   minutes over medium heat.
4. Add to cooked pinto beans and blend. Serve hot.

SERVES 6 TO 8

HACHAMORE HOMINY

This recipe will bring that hominy to life.

  4 tablespoons margarine
  1 large can cooked yellow hominy, drained
  2 green onions, chopped
  1 teaspoon salt
¹/₂ teaspoon black pepper
  1 8-ounce can sliced mushrooms, drained

1. Melt margarine in a skillet and add all ingredients.
2. Cook over medium heat stirring frequently until hominy is
   lightly browned.

SERVES 4

6

BRONCO BUSTIN' BREADS AND DESSERTS

CORRAL CORN BREAD

Hungry? Try this cowboy's delight—corral corn bread. A tradition around these parts.

1 cup yellow cornmeal
1 cup flour
1/2 cup sugar
4 tablespoons baking powder
1 cup milk or buttermilk
1 egg
1/4 cup vegetable oil

1. Preheat oven to 425°.
2. Combine all dry ingredients in a bowl.
3. Stir in wet ingredients and beat until fairly smooth.
4. Pour into an 8-inch baking pan and bake for 20 to 25 minutes.

SERVES 4 TO 6

CALIENTE CORN BREAD

This is a hot Tex-Mex dish on any menu.

  1 cup yellow cornmeal
 1/2 cup flour
 1/2 teaspoon baking soda
  4 tablespoons baking powder
 2/3 cup buttermilk
  2 eggs
 1/4 cup cream-style corn
  2 tablespoons vegetable oil
 1/4 cup chopped onion
 1/2 cup seeded and chopped jalapeño peppers
  1 cup grated cheddar cheese

1. Preheat oven to 400°.
2. Combine all dry ingredients in a bowl.
3. Stir in wet ingredients until fairly smooth.
4. Pour into a greased 10-inch skillet and bake for 30 minutes.

SERVES 4 TO 6

TRAILBLAZER BISCUITS

Round 'em up and head 'em out. Just the right flavored biscuits for the trail or at home. You can't be steered wrong with these.

2 cups flour
1 cup whole-wheat flour
4 tablespoons baking powder
3 tablespoons sugar
1/2 teaspoon salt
3/4 cup margarine
1 egg, beaten
1 cup milk

1. Preheat oven to 450°.
2. Combine dry ingredients in a bowl.
3. Stir in wet ingredients quickly.
4. Transfer dough to a floured board or wax paper. Knead lightly, then roll gently until 1 inch thick.
5. Cut dough into 1- to 2-inch biscuits and place in a 10-inch greased iron skillet or pan.
6. Bake for 12 to 15 minutes.

SERVES 4 TO 6

NOT-SO-QUIET HUSH PUPPIES

These hush puppies seem to bark out "Taste me." They're a flavor-packed treat. Bite into one.

2 cups yellow cornmeal
2 teaspoons baking powder
1 teaspoon salt
1 cup buttermilk
$1/2$ cup minced onions
$1/2$ teaspoon baking soda
1 egg
$1/8$ teaspoon celery salt
$1/8$ teaspoon garlic salt
$1/4$ teaspoon parsley flakes
2 cups vegetable oil

1. In a large bowl mix ingredients as listed, except oil, until well-blended.
2. Heat oil in a skillet, then drop batter by teaspoonful into hot oil.
3. Cook until golden brown over medium heat.

SERVES 4 TO 6

BUCKSKIN BREAD

This simple home-styled bread is baked with goodness in every slice.

2 cups flour
1 teaspoon baking powder
1 teaspoon salt
1 cup water

1. Preheat oven to 400°.
2. Sift flour, baking powder, and salt into a mixing bowl.
3. Mix in water.
4. Press dough into a greased 9-inch pie pan and bake for 25 minutes.

YIELDS 1 BREAD

MILK BREAD

Whip up this recipe for some smooth-tastin' bread.

  4 cups milk
  1 cup yellow cornmeal
  3 teaspoons salt
1½ teaspoons baking powder
  1 teaspoon sugar
  6 eggs, separated
  3 tablespoons margarine

1. In a saucepan bring milk to a rolling boil. Remove from heat. Preheat oven to 375°.
2. Add cornmeal, salt, baking powder, sugar, beaten egg yolks, and margarine.
3. Beat egg whites and fold into batter.
4. Pour batter into a greased baking pan and bake for about 30 minutes, until lightly brown.

YIELDS 1 BREAD

STRAWBERRY BREAD

Any way you slice it, this bread is delicious.

3 cups flour
1 teaspoon baking soda
1 teaspoon salt
1 teaspoon cinnamon
2 cups sugar
4 eggs, beaten
1¼ cups vegetable oil
2 cups sliced frozen strawberries, thawed
1½ cups chopped pecans

1. Preheat oven to 350°.
2. In a mixing bowl sift flour, baking soda, salt, cinnamon, and sugar together.
3. In a separate bowl mix eggs, oil, strawberries, and nuts.
4. Blend the two mixtures together, stirring just enough to make flour moist.
5. Pour into 5 greased bread pans and bake for 40 minutes.

YIELDS 5 OR 6 LOAVES

NUT BREAD

You'll be nuts about this bread.

2 cups flour
1 teaspoon salt
4 teaspoons baking powder
1 cup sugar
2 cups whole-wheat flour
2 cups milk
1 egg, beaten
1 cup chopped pecans
1/2 cup chopped dried figs or dates

1. In a mixing bowl sift first 4 ingredients together.
2. Mix in wheat flour.
3. Blend in milk, egg, nuts, and fruit.
4. Place in a greased bread pan and let stand 20 minutes. Meanwhile, preheat oven to 350°.
5. Bake for about 45 minutes.

YIELDS 1 LOAF

CARROT BREAD

Bet you didn't know that bread could taste so good.

 1 pound carrots, peeled and grated
³/₄ cup hot water
 1 cup cornmeal
1¹/₂ cups flour
 1 teaspoon baking powder
1¹/₂ teaspoons salt
 1 cup sugar
 2 tablespoons melted margarine
1¹/₄ cups warm milk
 2 tablespoons dark Karo syrup
 2 eggs, beaten

1. In a saucepan put carrots and water and simmer, covered, over medium heat for 15 minutes. Set aside in a strainer to drain.
2. Preheat oven to 400°. In a mixing bowl sift together cornmeal, flour, baking powder, salt, and sugar.
3. In a separate bowl combine margarine, milk, syrup, and eggs; mix into dry ingredients.
4. Shake and press all water from carrots and fold into batter.
5. Pour into a greased bread pan and bake for 1 hour.

YIELDS 1 LOAF

TEXAS AMBROSIA

You'll think you're in honky-tonk heaven when you sink your teeth into Texas Ambrosia.

 2 red apples, sliced into bite-size pieces
Juice of 1 lemon
 4 or 5 ripe oranges (navel preferred), peeled and sectioned
$3/4$ cup chopped pecans
$1^1/2$ cups crushed pineapple
$^1/2$ cup shredded coconut
$^1/2$ cup fresh cherries

1. Put apple pieces in a large bowl and squeeze lemon juice over them.
2. Add remaining fruit and nuts.
3. Chill and serve.

SERVES 6 TO 8

FIVE FRUIT AMBROSIA

This light dish makes a delightful confection.

2 cups sour cream
1 cup miniature marshmallows
1 cup sliced bananas
1 cup chunked pineapples
1 apple, diced
1 cup mandarin orange sections
1/2 cup Maraschino cherries
1/2 cup chopped pecans

Combine all ingredients in a bowl. Chill thoroughly before serving.

SERVES 6 TO 8

PEACH COBBLER

A real sweet peach of a treat.

1/2 cup melted margarine
1/2 cup sugar
1/2 cup milk
1/2 cup flour
1 teaspoon baking powder
4 cups sliced frozen peaches, thawed

1. Preheat oven to 375°.
2. In a bowl mix all ingredients except peaches until smooth.
3. Pour batter into a baking pan and add peaches, but don't stir them in.
4. Bake for 30 minutes, or until crust rises to the top and browns lightly.

YIELDS 1 COBBLER

BLUEBERRY BUCKLE

Be careful. Too many Blueberry Buckles just might make you unbuckle your buckle.

3/4 cup sugar
1/4 cup soft butter
 1 egg
1/2 cup milk
 2 cups flour
 2 teaspoons baking powder
1/2 teaspoon salt
 2 cups frozen blueberries, thawed and well-drained

CRUMB MIXTURE
1/2 cup sugar
1/3 cup flour
1/2 teaspoon cinnamon
1/4 cup softened butter

1. Preheat oven to 375°.
2. In a bowl mix together sugar, butter, and egg.
3. Stir in milk, flour, baking powder, and salt.
4. Carefully fold in blueberries.
5. Prepare crumb mixture by blending in a separate bowl.
6. Pour batter into a greased square baking pan and sprinkle crumb mixture on top.
7. Bake for 45 to 50 minutes.

YIELDS NINE 3-INCH SQUARES

BLACKBERRY PUDDING

Try this blackberry pudding and you can raise the roof on any honky-tonk.

 1 cup flour
 2 cups sugar
1/8 teaspoon salt
3/4 cup milk
1 1/2 teaspoons baking powder
1/2 cup melted margarine
 1 cup frozen blackberries, thawed
 1 cup cold water
1/8 teaspoon nutmeg

1. Preheat oven to 375°.
2. In a bowl mix flour, 1 cup sugar, salt, milk, and baking powder.
3. Pour melted margarine into a baking pan.
4. Pour batter into pan over margarine (do not stir).
5. In a bowl mix berries, water, 1 cup sugar, and nutmeg together; pour over batter (do not stir).
6. Bake for 45 minutes. Cool.

SERVES 4 TO 6

TEXAS SWEET RICE PUDDING

Share a bowl of Texas rice pudding with that special someone.

 3 cups cooked rice
 3 eggs, beaten
 1/2 cup honey
2 1/2 cups milk
 1 teaspoon vanilla
 1/8 teaspoon nutmeg
 1/8 teaspoon cinnamon

1. Preheat oven to 325°.
2. Combine ingredients in a 2-quart casserole.
3. Bake for 30 minutes, stir, and bake another 30 minutes. Serve warm or cold.

SERVES 4 TO 6

COWBOY CUSTARD

A real cowboy would trade his horse for a taste of this custard.

 2 cups cream-style corn
 1 tablespoon butter
 1/2 teaspoon salt
 2 teaspoons baking powder
 1 tablespoon cornstarch
 2 eggs, well-beaten
 1/2 cup milk

1. Preheat oven to 350°.
2. In a bowl combine all ingredients and mix well.
3. Pour into a well-greased pie pan and bake for 30 minutes.

SERVES 4 TO 6

STANDARD PIE SHELL

1 cup sifted flour
1/2 teaspoon salt
1/3 plus 1 tablespoon lard or shortening
2 tablespoons water

1. Preheat oven to 425°.
2. In a bowl mix flour and salt together.
3. Cut in lard or shortening until blended.
4. Slowly add water, mixing with a fork.
5. Press into a ball and roll out on a lightly floured board.
6. Place dough into a 9-inch pie pan and cut edges to fit pan.
7. Bake for 8 to 10 minutes.

YIELDS ONE 9-INCH SHELL

PECAN PIE

3 eggs, separated
1/4 teaspoon salt
1 cup dark Karo syrup
3/4 cup sugar
3 tablespoons melted butter
1 teaspoon vanilla
1 cup pecan pieces
1 unbaked Standard Pie Shell (see opposite page) or
   store-bought 9-inch shell

1. Preheat oven to 400°.
2. In a large bowl beat egg whites and salt until stiff.
3. Add syrup, sugar, butter, and vanilla and continue to beat.
4. Fold in pecans.
5. Pour batter into raw pie shell and bake for 10 minutes, then lower heat to 350° for 25 to 30 minutes.

SERVES 8 TO 10

SERVING SUGGESTION: Serve with whipped cream or ice cream.

GOODTIME STRAWBERRY PIE

Anytime is a good time when you serve this tasty delight.

   1 cup fresh strawberries
   4 tablespoons sugar
   2 egg yolks
   1 can condensed milk
   3 ounces cream cheese
½ cup lemon juice
   1 pint whipping cream

1. Cut up fresh strawberries, add sugar, and let sit for about 30 minutes.
2. Blend egg yolks, milk, cream cheese, and lemon juice. Carefully, add strawberries.
3. Whip whipping cream for toppings.
4. Put strawberry mixture in baked pie shell and add topping.
5. Refrigerate and serve cool.

CHESS PIE

3 egg yolks, beaten

1$\frac{1}{3}$ tablespoons flour

$\frac{2}{3}$ cup sugar

$\frac{1}{4}$ teaspoon salt

1 teaspoon vanilla

1$\frac{1}{3}$ cups cream

1 cup cut-up dates

1 cup raisins

1 cup chopped walnuts

1. Preheat oven to 350°.
2. In a bowl combine yolks, flour, sugar, salt, and vanilla.
3. Fold in cream, dates, raisins, and nuts.
4. Pour into raw pie shell and bake for 50 to 60 minutes.

SERVES 8 TO 10

YAHOO YAM CUSTARD PIE

You'll toss up your six-gallon and shoot off your six-shooter when you slice up this pie.

2   cups cold, mashed, cooked yams
3   egg yolks
1/2 cup brown sugar
1/3 cup melted butter
1/2 teaspoon salt
1   cup canned milk
1   unbaked Standard Pie Shell (page 144) or store-bought 9-inch shell

TOPPING
3   egg whites
1/2 cup white sugar
1/2 teaspoon vanilla

1. Preheat oven to 350°.
2. In a large bowl beat yams and egg yolks together until well mixed.
3. Beat in brown sugar, butter, salt, and canned milk.
4. Pour into raw pie shell and bake for 40 minutes.
5. Meanwhile, prepare topping: In a bowl beat egg whites until fluffy.
6. Slowly add in white sugar and continue to beat until stiff; add vanilla.
7. Remove pie from oven and spoon topping over it.
8. Return to oven and bake at 425° for 5 minutes.

SERVES 8 TO 10

GILLEY'S COUNTRY PIE

Wherever you're at, you're in Gilley's Country when you try this pie.

  1 *cup plus 2 tablespoons sugar*
  1 *cup sour cream*
 $1/2$ *cup raisins*
 $1/2$ *teaspoon cinnamon*
 $1/2$ *teaspoon cloves*
  2 *eggs, separated*
  1 *unbaked Standard Pie Shell (page 144) or store-bought 9-inch shell*

1. Preheat oven to 350°.
2. In a bowl combine 1 cup sugar, sour cream, raisins, cinnamon, cloves, and egg yolks, blending well.
3. Pour into raw pie shell and bake for 20 minutes.
4. In a bowl beat egg whites and 2 tablespoons sugar to make meringue.
5. Remove pie from oven, top with meringue, and bake briefly, until lightly browned.

SERVES 8 TO 10

SYRUP PIE

This pie tastes as sweet as it looks, and it will mellow even the wildest cowboy.

1³/₄ cups sugar
1¹/₂ tablespoons flour
 5 eggs, separated
 1 cup dark Karo syrup
 1 cup sweet cream
 1 tablespoon margarine
¹/₂ teaspoon cinnamon
¹/₂ teaspoon cloves
¹/₂ teaspoon nutmeg
¹/₈ teaspoon salt
 1 unbaked Standard Pie Shell (page 144) or store-bought 10-inch shell

1. Preheat oven to 375°.
2. In a bowl mix 1¹/₂ cups sugar, flour, and beaten egg yolks until smooth.
3. Stir in syrup, cream, margarine, spices, and ¹/₁₆ teaspoon salt.
4. Pour batter into raw pie shell and bake for 35 minutes or until firm.
5. In another bowl beat egg whites until stiff and add ¹/₄ cup sugar slowly.
6. Add ¹/₁₆ teaspoon salt and beat until meringue is stiff.
7. Remove pie from oven, cover with meringue, and bake briefly at 300° until lightly browned.

SERVES 8 TO 10

FUDGE CAKE

Sink your teeth into fudge cake and you'll know what heaven is all about.

¹/₂ cup melted margarine
4 ounces unsweetened chocolate
1 cup sugar
3 eggs, separated
1 cup chopped pecans
1 teaspoon vanilla
³/₄ cup flour
1 teaspoon baking powder

1. Preheat oven to 350°.
2. Melt margarine and chocolate together in a saucepan and let cool.
3. Add in sugar, beaten egg yolks, pecans, and vanilla, and beat until smooth.
4. Sift flour and baking powder into batter and mix well.
5. Beat egg whites in a separate bowl, and fold in.
6. Pour batter into a greased baking pan (about 8 inches square) and bake for 25 minutes until done.

SERVES 6 TO 8

TEXAS DELIGHT CHOCOLATE CAKE

A classic dessert treat and everybody's favorite.

  1 *cup buttermilk*
2¹/₂ *cups sugar*
  1 *cup butter*
  3 *cups cake flour*
  4 *teaspoons cocoa*
  1 *teaspoon salt*
  5 *tablespoons strong coffee*
  1 *teaspoon baking soda*
  2 *tablespoons vanilla*
  5 *egg whites, beaten until stiff*

1. Preheat oven to 275°F.
2. Prepare four 8-inch round layer pans.
3. Blend butter, milk, sugar, and butter in mixing bowl; add all other ingredients.
4. Divide batter evenly into the four greased pans.
5. Bake 30 minutes.
6. Cool on wire racks.

SERVES 8 TO 12

TEXAS DELIGHT CHOCOLATE ICING

1 *cup butter at room temperature*
1 *box confectioner's sugar*
1 *egg yolk*
2 *tablespoons cocoa*
1 *tablespoon vanilla*
3 *tablespoons strong coffee*

1. Blend butter and sugar in sauce pan.
2. Add egg yolk and stir.
3. Add all other ingredients.
4. Cook while stirring at low heat until thickened.

FILLS AND FROSTS FOUR 8-INCH LAYERS

LONE STAR APPLESAUCE CAKE

Be the star of your kitchen with this Lone Star Applesauce Cake.

$^1/_2$ cup butter
 1 cup brown sugar
 1 egg, beaten
 1 cup fresh or canned applesauce
$1^3/_4$ cups flour
 1 teaspoon baking soda
$^1/_2$ teaspoon nutmeg
 1 teaspoon cinnamon
$^1/_2$ teaspoon salt
$^3/_4$ cup seedless raisins
$^1/_4$ cup chopped walnuts

1. Preheat oven to 350°.
2. In a bowl cream butter until soft.
3. Blend in brown sugar, then add in egg.
4. Stir in remaining ingredients, blending well.
5. Turn batter into a greased 8-inch loaf pan and bake for about 45 minutes.

SERVES 8 TO 10

OATMEAL COOKIES

An old-fashioned treat that's on everyone's list of favorites.

1/2 cup melted margarine
 1 teaspoon nutmeg
 1 cup sugar
 2 eggs
 2 cups oatmeal
1/2 cup chopped pecans

1. Preheat oven to 350°.
2. In a bowl blend margarine, nutmeg, and sugar.
3. Mix in eggs one at a time and beat well.
4. Blend in oatmeal and pecans thoroughly.
5. Drop batter from teaspoon onto a greased cookie sheet and bake for about 15 minutes, until golden brown.

YIELDS APPROXIMATELY 3 DOZEN COOKIES

WHISKEY PLUGS

This treat is strong and sweet—packs quite a wallop!

 3 cups crumbled vanilla wafers
 1 cup chopped pecans
1/2 cup Southern Comfort whiskey
 1 cup confectioners' sugar
 3 tablespoons light Karo syrup
1 1/2 tablespoons cocoa

1. Combine all ingredients in a bowl and mix well.
2. Roll into 1-inch balls and dust lightly with extra confectioners' sugar. Serve as is or chill first.

YIELDS ABOUT 2 DOZEN "PLUGS"

Index